Home Gardening

EDITED BY ARTHUR DENMARSH

Home Gardening

EDITED BY ARTHUR DENMARSH

THE WARWICK PRESS

Contributors

Ronald Blom

Jack Harkness

Ronald Menage

John Negus

Barry Phillips

Betty Rochford

Tom Rochford

Brian Walkden

Ian Walls

Stanley Whitehead

Contents

1 Garden Design

Designing a garden is a fascinating occupation but it calls for a lot of patience and while it is sometimes excitingly rewarding it is often frustratingly disappointing.

Very few people can choose what they consider the ideal site for a garden, whether it's an existing garden or merely a rectangle of land left by the builder; a sea of mud and lumps of brick and concrete. Most of us have to live near our work and acquire the house that is available and within our means. The exceptions are the retired people who may be able to live where they choose but the majority of us have to come to terms with what we've got and a compromise must be reached between the ideal and the reality. It's no good pining for a garden of rhododendrons and azaleas unless your soil is lime free nor striving after superb roses and delphiniums if you have a light, acid soil.

What sort of a garden do you want? If you are young, with small children, a garden that can be played in without causing too much damage will save a lot of heartbreak and scolding. Balls don't always go where they are hit or kicked and broken glass and smashed tulips will result in tears. Much the same applies to animals. Little children love sandpits, climbing frames and swings and while these may not improve the view from the house it saves mother a lot of worry if she can watch the family at play. If there is space for a terrace this is always worthwhile; meals outside in the summer; a

The plants in a garden and their arrangement should complement the house to which they belong

place for a pram; even a play area when the grass is damp.

On the other hand if you are retired you must face the fact that at 85 you won't feel as energetic as you do at 65 and a lot of mowing, hedge trimming and fiddly weeding will be a tiring chore. After all, gardens are for relaxing, so think ahead and aim for more flowering shrubs and plants that need no staking. Consider a raised flower bed that will save kneeling and a small greenhouse will provide hours of happy occupation.

The boundary of your garden is probably the first consideration. It may already exist. If not it can be a wall, a fence, a hedge or just wire netting. To inherit a wall is wonderful. To build one is costly because to be of real value it needs to be at least 2m/6ft high; but there are so many marvellous plants that will grow up a wall or under its protection. There are a number of composition blocks on the market from which it is possible to construct a highly decorative and very satisfactory wall at less cost than using bricks and the great advantage is that it needs no maintenance. From the gardener's point of view a fence is probably the next best thing. It doesn't take up a lot of space; it is easy to fix things to and it keeps out the next door weeds. It will need a certain amount of maintenance and will not last a lifetime. Hedges make delightful backgrounds to herbaceous borders but they have disadvantages. They have to be kept cut; they tend to grow 60–90cm/24–36in wide; weeds lodge at their roots and they take a lot of goodness from the soil around them. A wire fence is fine if you don't object to your

Left: a sunken sandpit can provide privacy as well as safety for a small child
Below: a patio garden showing plenty of variety

neighbours' weeds, cats or children's toys coming through, or if you don't mind a lack of privacy. Plants can grow close to it and climbers trail over it so that in summer, at least, it will be more or less invisible.

The largest area of any garden is usually the lawn. It is very much simpler to mow in straight lines so a simple rectangle makes for least work, but it is also rather dull and a pleasantly curved edge to the grass seems to make the area look larger. The thing that really makes for hard work is a lot of little beds cut into the lawn or single trees and shrubs that have to be mown round.

Everyone is fascinated by water and a garden with natural water is a delight but small ponds have drawbacks. A toddler can fall, hit its head on a stone and drown in a few inches of water. If this is not a problem there are many charming plants for a water garden and the sound of a little, bubbling fountain is very pleasant on a hot day. For fuller details of water and its uses, see page 95.

Rockeries are a very popular garden feature. They can be extremely beautiful, especially in spring, if they are well constructed and designed to fit into the contours of the garden but they can all too easily become a jumble of any available rocks and stones, piled together with no thought as to the strata of the rock nor the need for leaving suitable areas for planting. If you want a rockery consult someone who really knows or make a careful study of it before you start to build – we tell you the basic information on page 87. Weeding a rockery can be a problem. Roots get wedged under rocks or entwined with a spreading mass of rock plant. A peat garden, built of peat blocks, might be a simpler alternative, and it offers a wonderful opportunity for growing a wide variety of fascinating and unusual plants.

A vegetable garden, however small, is a very

If you have a cat, some precious plants will need protection from it

A well-stocked border which will give interest and colour throughout the year

good idea, even if it only produces lettuces and herbs. With a large family and a small garden unless you are prepared to give up most of the ground it is hardly worthwhile attempting to grow more than salad crops and herbs but two people can grow enough for their needs in quite a small space.

Having decided on the type of layout you want don't be too impatient. Make quite sure you know which parts of the garden get full sunshine and which areas are shady and, if possible, whether you have any frost pockets. Your house will probably face at least partially south so that the area opposite the house will face north and will not get so much sun. You will want shade but site any tree you plant carefully and make sure that you know how big it will grow. A weeping willow–charmingly delicate when young–will all too quickly develop a twenty foot

spread and a silver birch will grow to 15m/50ft. There are plenty of small trees to choose from. Evergreens and conifers, used sparingly, give colour in the winter and there are many very attractive dwarf varieties of conifer in all shades of green.

Shrubs are labour saving and carefully chosen will provide colour throughout the year. If they are planted in groups, 'bays' can be left for herbaceous plants, bulbs and annuals.

It is an excellent idea to go round any gardens in your district that are open and look at what your neighbours grow successfully. One can get good ideas from other peoples' successful planting and owners and gardeners are usually only too happy to share their knowledge and experience. Wherever possible buy from a local nursery or garden centre as the plants will have been raised in similar conditions. Make sure that you know the maximum size of what you are buying and remember that plants don't grow very much for the first two years but that then they will suddenly get big. It's so much easier to add new plants than to decide what to dig up and the gaps can always be filled with bulbs and annuals.

When planting a garden there are a few points worth bearing in mind. Straight lines look horrible unless you want a totally formal and immaculately kept garden or go in for carpet bedding. Groups of flowers of the same kind or of the same colour make a far greater impact than single blobs of colour and three plants triangled together will not only support each other but if one fails to do well the others will help fill the gap.

Blue and mauve are colours that will fade into the background and can give an impression of depth while white and yellow flowers 'come forward' and will shine against a dark background.

Colour combinations are very much a matter of taste and while no colours in nature can be said to clash some are certainly more effective

Above: a small garden carefully designed to provide privacy

Below: a spring view

Below: an irregularly shaped lawn gives an illusion of space

together than others. If you can imagine the colours of the rainbow; violet, indigo, blue, green, yellow, orange and red carefully graded into each other and forming a circle you will find that any colour will blend well with the colours next to it and make a splendid contrast with the colour diametrically opposite.

Think, too, in terms of seasons. A group of spring flowers will look much more striking than a patch here and there and a small area devoted to winter flowering plants will be much more noticeable than peering for little bits all over the place. A small conifer, some winter flowering heathers and a plant or two of the lovely green *Helleborus foetidus* will give colour on dark days and last well into the spring.

Daffodils are a joy. We can't all have orchards full of them, though where possible they look best coming naturally out of grass. Keep them in loose clumps so that grass or soil shows between them. They will look much prettier than in a solid yellow mass. Don't be afraid to plant your early flowering plants and bulbs at the back of a border. The other plants will not have grown big enough to hide them and when they are over you won't be left with an untidy patch in the front.

If you love tiny, unusual plants that are such fun to collect, keep a special place where they can all grow together otherwise they get lost and dug up or overtaken by larger neighbours.

If the site on which your garden is to be made already has some natural feature, an old tree, or a mound or hollow, leave it, if possible. It will look much more attractive than something 'contrived'. An old fruit tree may not produce much fruit but the blossom will be lovely and a *Clematis montana* or *Rosa filipes* will romp through branches.

2 Climate

The relationships between the surrounding physical conditions (the climate) and the growth of plants is very complex and by no means fully understood. Nevertheless it is important that a good gardener should appreciate the principles involved.

First of all there is the general climate of the area where you live, the details of which will be found in officially published statistics. The next is the local climate, which is a further modification of the general conditions – for instance if you live at the bottom of a hill, you are more likely to experience frosts than your neighbours at the top because cool air travels downhill. Finally there is the microclimate, the exact conditions surrounding each growing plant, and over which you can exert some influence – a screen against wind, a delicate plant on the sheltered side of a more hardy specimen, and so on.

Main Weather Conditions

The most important forms of weather which will affect your plants are soil moisture, sunlight and temperature. Wind is also important.

Soil Moisture

Plants need moist soil to enable their roots to take up the essential nutrients from the earth. Soils vary in the amount of moisture they can hold. Coarse sandy soil drains very fast indeed, and you will need to add lots of water holding humus; rich soils can hold up to twice as much moisture as sandy, and will make watering a less arduous task.

Sunlight

Sunshine provides energy and light. Different plants need very considerably different amounts of light and shade, and it is important to match the plant with its appropriate conditions in your garden when you plant it. The sunniest places in the British Isles are those nearest the coast, and especially the south and south west. On higher ground there will be less hours of sun.

In summer, plants transpire water in hot sunny weather, and nearly all gardens will need the water balancing maintaining by artificial irrigation.

Rainfall

The best rainfall from the point of view of a garden is that which occurs fairly steadily throughout the year. Not very much will survive months of drought followed by torrential monsoon-type rains. The UK is a good place for a gardener for this reason, although some years will always be exceptional for the amount of rainfall or the lack of it.

Temperature

The temperature of the air and the soil in which a plant lives are of vital importance in its development. Temperature controls the rate, if at all, at which seeds germinate, the period when the leaves give way to flowers and fruit, and the progress towards maturity.

Average temperatures decrease with the height of the ground above sea level, so that if you live in a hilly area you must accept that you will not have the same choice of outdoor plants as those lower down. On the other hand, there

Above left: witch hazel in winter
Above: a winter scene
Below left: five different ways of
protecting plants

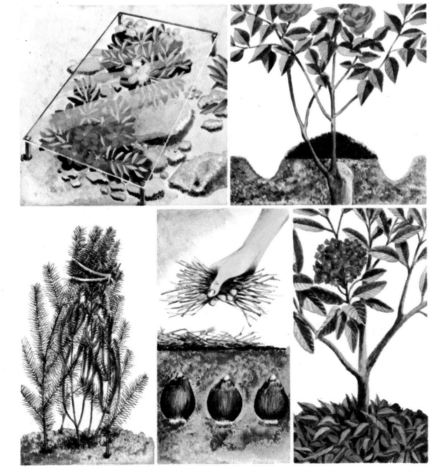

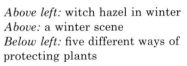

are plenty of plants which actually prefer cool conditions.

Very cold winters are the worst threat to all other than annual plants, and the worst problems occur when a mild spell which encourages plants to start into growth is followed by a sudden return to wintry conditions. It is always worthwhile having sacks, polythene sheets and cloches available to protect tender plants at short notice.

The temperature in summer will determine whether a plant will reach full maturity; warmth is as important for most plants as is the length of the growing season.

Frost

Frost causes two different kinds of damage. It can break the plant tissues, or it can freeze the moisture in the ground and thus prevent it reaching the roots. The average date of the last frost in any area is an unreliable guide to the

Above: poppies are always popular
Below: a seaside climate is good for many plants

time at which you can plant out tender subjects. If you do not know your area well, ask around amongst the neighbours or at a local college, and see if they are able to tell you the frost patterns in the area. Of course you cannot wait for ever to plant out your half-hardy and tender plants; it is almost certain to happen sooner or later that some will be caught by an unusually late or severe frost. A little local knowledge though should mean that planting out is successful in most seasons.

The simplest way to protect your plants against frost is to keep the soil moist, free from weeds and as compact as possible. This will mean that heat rises during the night, thus warding off frost.

Wind

Everyone has seen the damage to fields, trees and hedges caused by gales, but even moderate winds can cause considerable havoc in a garden. If your garden is small, hedges will give the best protection if they are placed to the windward side of the plot. If you have a larger area, tree shelter belts will perform the same function even more effectively. Hedges and trees provide shelter for a distance of about seven times their height; if you have room for neither, and have to settle for a wall or fence, this will give you protection to a distance of five times its height.

Shelter is always most necessary near the coast where off-sea winds cause heavy damage.

Climate in Detail

A very full and detailed description of the regional climate of England and Wales is given in *Technical Bulletin No 35* of the Ministry of Agriculture, Fisheries and Food, called 'The Agricultural Climate of England and Wales', published by Her Majesty's Stationery Office.

3 Garden Tools and their Maintenance

For most aspects of gardening, tools and equipment of one sort or another are essential. Choice is dictated, not only by the size and nature of the garden, but the physical attributes of the gardener. This is especially true when it comes to a choice between manual and motorized equipment. One always tends to start with what might be called basic necessities.

Spades

Spades are for digging, cultivating and moving soil, sand and other growing materials, although a shovel, with its larger surface, is more effective for the latter. To use a spade properly, it is inserted vertically into the soil, a portion of soil removed, and replaced with the soil inverted. This is done with a flicking action. It may be necessary to strip off turf or weeds before ground is dug, cutting this over with a scythe or mower beforehand, if need be.

The first thing to do when you go to buy a spade is find one which looks the right size and pick it up and see if you can handle it easily. The smaller size of spade is a 'border' spade and they then get numbered from 1 to 4. Most men of reasonable strength can handle a number 2 or 3, whereas for a lady, a 'border' spade or a number 1 is large enough. The quality of space you get depends on the price, the best spades being half bright or chrome finish, which slips through the soil with ease and requires the minimum of maintenance.

Forks

These are for forking over the ground, loosening it up, handling manure and so on. Lighter types

Always clean tools and put them away after use

of soil can, in fact, be turned over reasonably well with forks, using much the same action as with digging–although an open trench is not necessary. There are digging forks with square prongs, and potato forks with flat prongs on one side and manure forks which have very sharp metal prongs, and are dangerous instruments to have around. The same size formula applies as for spades.

Barrows

A wheelbarrow of one kind or another for transporting weeds and garden rubbish is a must. The popular type has a galvanized metal body with an action roller bearing wheel. Tyres can be either solid or pneumatic, the latter being

A barrow, with spade, secateurs and gardening gloves

A selection of lawn care equipment

better for use on soft land. The traditional barrow has one wheel and two handles, although there are bogey types of barrows around which can be useful, especially for people who are partly disabled.

Rakes

Many types of rakes are available, ranging from the ordinary metal tooth type to the large aluminium or wooden rake. Another type is the flexible wire rake, handy for raking up leaves, stirring surfaces of lawns. The 'normal' type of rake is used for raking land level and preparing it for sowing, and a little experience will show that, while the aluminium lightweight rakes are more expensive to buy, they are easier to work with, and give an excellent finish, as they do not dig into the soil. They are also easier to maintain and will last well.

Gardening Lines with Reel and Pin

It is almost impossible to sow or plant straight rows of anything without a good line. The reel and pin portions are best made of alloy, which gives them a long life and avoids rusting, whereas the line itself is usually polypropylene or nylon. A simple line can be made with two sticks and a length of string.

Hoes

Like rakes, there are many different types, from the traditional Dutch and draw-hoes, to the more sophisticated shapes. The modern types of hoes are very light and strong and a pleasure to use. Hoes are used for weeding and taking out seed drills, also the earthing up of plants, such as potatoes.

Picks

Especially for the new garden, some form of pick is a basic item, being ideal for dealing with hard baked land or for levering out of bricks and stones half-buried in the soil.

Other fairly basic items are spirit levels for finding true levels for paths, greenhouses, bases and the like. A saw, preferably of the narrow bladed type, called a pruning saw. A garden riddle of about half inch mesh (10–12mm) for riddling soil, sand, ashes etc. A plastic watering can and a general purpose pressure spray for applying weedkillers are really essential items, the latter especially for cleaning up soil with weedkillers or dealing with pests and diseases. Some gardeners like to keep separate sprays for weedkillers and pesticides – but if the sprayer is *washed out carefully with warm water after use* – there is not a great deal of risk. A trowel

Small tools for work in crowded parts of the garden

and a fork, preferably of superior finish, to avoid rapid deterioration, cannot be managed without in any garden. A garden knife for taking cuttings – pruning – should be in every gardener's pocket. A pair of secateurs which should be of good quality, as cheaper types tend to deteriorate very quickly, is needed fairly constantly in all gardens. A pair of edging shears for trimming lawn edges, and hedge shears for hedge trimming, are required sooner or later. These can vary considerably in design and here again, quality is important, although weight factor should be taken into account, as a heavy pair of shears can be tiring to use. A hose-pipe is also fairly basic in most gardens.

Lawnmowers

A massive range of lawnmowers are available today. First of all, it is necessary to decide on the size and nature of the area of grass to be cut, whether it is to be kept finely mown or left rough. Of vital importance is who will do the cutting, as some of the heavier types of mowers can be difficult to operate by a woman.

The cheapest forms of small lawnmowers of the manual kind are those of side wheel design, where the grass is cut by blades driven from one of the side wheels. The cheaper the mower, the fewer the cuts to the yard or metre, this being dependent on the number of cutting blades and the gearing between the drive wheel and the cylinder. The smaller side wheel mowers have the advantage of being light to handle and they give a perfectly adequate finish and can be ideal for the unbroken lawn of up to about $50–90\text{m}^2$/60–100 sq yds. The weakness of the side wheel machine is in cutting edges, something they cannot effectively do. On the other hand, they are often better for badly sloping land.

The roller type of manual machine gives a better finish and usually at about 50–60 cuts m/yd. They are better for good surface lawns and where there are a lot of edges involved, as the roller stops the mower falling over the edge.

Whether or not to buy a powered mower, driven either by electricity or petrol, depends on a number of factors. Large areas of grass almost certainly will demand power mowers.

Recent years have seen a tremendous increase in the number of rotary cutters as opposed to those which cut on a horizontal plane. The finish they give is excellent, and they are certainly better for rougher grass areas, especially where the land is sloping and where there are a lot of trees planted up in the grass. Hovercraft types of mowers are specially good for rough, undulating ground, but all rotary type mowers must be used with considerable care, *especially the hovercraft types.*

Rotary Cultivators

Like lawnmowers, these have been the subject of considerable design and improvement in the last decade. Whether or not the expense of buying one is justified, depends very much on the area of ground to be constantly recultivated each year. It might, in fact, be perfectly adequate to hire a cultivator for initial cultivation of a new garden, or even once a year. On the other hand, rotary cultivators are excellent for inter-row cultivation between more widely grown crops, such as raspberries, strawberries, soft fruit. It is true to say, however, that modern weed-killers can take away much of the effort of cultivating ground purely for weed control. It should be

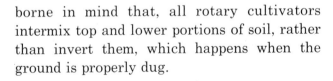

Above left: watering equipment
Above right: mending a hose-pipe
Below left: equipment for the indoor gardener
Below right: a lawn fertilizer spreader

borne in mind that, all rotary cultivators intermix top and lower portions of soil, rather than invert them, which happens when the ground is properly dug.

Additional Tools
As the intensity of gardening increases, so will the need for more specialized tools arise. Such items are: fertilizer distributors (for lawns and pre-sowing or planting vegetables); spikers or aerators for lawns; irrigation equipment for lawns and the garden generally; seed drillers–mobile tool racks, electric hedge cutters (mains and battery type), mechanical edgers for lawns (generally electric), loppers for tall trees.

If you have a greenhouse, 'outside' tools will suffice, except for one very important tool–a dibber.

Maintenance of Tools and Equipment
Hand tools demand reasonable cleaning after use, storage under cover, and preferably, all metal surfaces coated with oil or grease during long periods of non-use. Leaving tools out of doors for long periods, especially during winter, leads to very rapid deterioration. Mechanical equipment, especially if power driven, must be serviced regularly. Cutting items, lawnmowers, shears and the like, should be sharpened and set professionally, before the commencement of each season.

4 Your Soil and how to Cultivate it

Plants and the Soil

Broadly, garden plants consist of two different but integrated structural systems–the above-ground system of stems, branches, green leaves, flowers and seeds; and the below-ground system of roots and root hairs, arranged about a common axis. Though complementary, the root system is fundamentally the more important to plant performance.

Apart from anchoring a plant in its environment, it has to supply it with water to sustain its functions and growth, and with a wide range of nutrient mineral elements, largely as soluble salts, to help form cell and organic structures and enable its leaves to manufacture foodstuffs photosynthetically for further healthy function and growth.

This flow of watery nutrient solution or sap from root hair to leaf cell influences growth profoundly, and in quality and quantity is decided by the ease with which the roots can penetrate the soil and tap its resources. In turn this depends upon the nature and condition of the soil; the thin surface skin of earth on which plant, animal and human life depends.

Soils and Their Nature

Individual soils will vary considerably in composition, texture, structure, colour and kind, but have five properties in common: 1) a mineral content of rock particles of very variable sizes, 2) an organic content of humus forming from dead and decomposing remains of plants and animals, 3) water from rains, 4) air filtering in and through from the atmosphere, and 5) a flora and fauna of tiny plants, algae and fungi, and of bacteria, micro-organisms, earthworms and insects. From the ferment of their biological and chemical interactivity comes the capacity of a soil to nurture plant growth, or its fertility.

The dominant and permanent part of a soil is its mineral content. It usually consists of a mixture of particles varying in sizes from stones and gravel, through coarse and fine gritty sands, smoother, silky silt to the very fine mud smearing particles of clay. The mineral particles, by their kind and proportions, determine the texture of a soil, and soils are classified accordingly.

Soil particles vary in shape as well as size. They do not lie solidly close together. There are interstices or spaces, known as the pore space, through which roots grow, and air and water circulate. The larger the soil particles, the larger the spaces between; the more quickly water percolates and drains through, and the more easily roots can grow, and the more readily they absorb warmth from the sun and lose it again.

For convenience mineral particles are classed as 1) stones and gravels when larger than 2mm in diameter; 2) sands when less than 2mm but greater than 0.02mm; 3) silt when less than 0.02mm but greater than 0.002mm; and 4) clay when less than 0.002mm down to ultra-microscopic sizes. They are an important source of mineral elements needed by plants. But whereas gravels, sands and silt are rather inert and very slowly soluble, clay is different. Its minute particles are more chemically active, and when wetted become colloidal or glue-like and hold soluble plant nutrients well. Any soil containing clay is inherently more fertile than one without.

Soils are designated according to the class of particles most predominant in their mineral make-up. Soils containing 80 per cent or more by weight of the coarser particles are either stony, gravelly or sandy. They are light and easy to work, open-pored, drain readily of moisture, and are well-aerated. Soils containing 20 per cent or more of the finest particles are clayey, heavy to work, fine-pored, dense, sticky, retentive of moisture, ill-aerated and slow to warm under the sun.

Soils containing little sand or clay but a preponderance of fine particles are silts, with fine pore spaces, lacking the openness of sand and the stickiness of clay, tending to consolidate inert, infertile and unresponsive unless well managed.

The better balanced the mineral matrix, however, the less extreme the soil characteristics, and it is termed a loam, though it may be a sandy loam, a clay loam or a silt loam, according to which group of particles remains most influential in its texture.

The Organic Content
The purely mineral part of a soil is infertile and cannot nurture garden plants. It needs an organic content, derived from the dead remains of plants, animals and myriads of micro-organisms accumulating and actively decomposing in the soil. This material is food for numerous soil organisms and bacteria which break it down into small fibrous particles and brown and black amorphous substances known as humus.

The organisms—bacteria, minute fungi, earthworms—themselves excrete compounds of value to plant life, release nutrient elements from the organic matter, and in dying decompose and perpetuate the build-up of a soil's organic content.

The fine fibres and organic particles help to fill in the large pore spaces between the larger mineral particles, and being absorbent, slow the movement and loss of water and soluble nutrients from the soil. But the key to soil fertility is humus. This is a highly complex substance or entity; largely composed of colloidal particles, extremely minute, and forming a gel that can enter all pore space, and transform inert soil into a biochemically reactive living earth.

Physically, it acts as a weak cement, grouping mineral particles together, particularly those of clay, into crumbs or granular structure. When wetted it swells and holds moisture to the benefit of open sandy soils, while in clay its formation of crumb structures or aggregates of soil particles improves aeration and drainage. Humus also darkens soils, so that they absorb the sun's heat more readily and retain it longer.

Biologically, humus is a centre of micro-organic activity; chemically it excites the release of soluble elements from all soil particles, and is itself a reservoir of nutrient for plants which roots reach into and exploit. Eventually, humus itself is broken down to simpler residues, such as nitrogen and carbonic acid, and disappears. Other things being equal, the more humus a soil contains, the more fertile it is. Unlike the mineral matrix, the organic content of a soil is subject to fluctuation, and under cultivation, usually needs building up.

The Role of Lime
Another critical factor in soil fertility and plant growth is the soil's content of lime. Lime controls the acid-alkaline balance in the soil and of the nutrient soil solution on which plant roots feed. Rains percolating through the soil slowly but steadily leach or wash lime out, and it becomes more acid. Increasing acidity is discouraging to the activity of many soil organisms breaking down organic matter. It is also detrimental to the growth of most garden plants and crops, with the exception of certain plants, chiefly rhododendrons and related members of the Ericaceae or Heath family, native to acid, lime-free soils. Most garden plants grow best where the soil contains some

A Quick Guide to Soils – Their Characteristics and Their Needs

Type of soil	Identifiable characteristics	Good points	Bad points	Treatments needed for Improvement
Stony, gravel	Many small to large stones in thin layer of soil	Good drainage from surface	Dries out too quickly Hard to work Poor fertility	Remove larger stones that hinder working Break up ground to give more rooting depth Feed liberally with humus-forming organic matter Use slow-acting fertilizers for base feeding
Sandy	Feels gritty to fingers Does not hold together when compressed Tends to be light in colour	Light to work Warms readily for early cropping Drains quickly	Dries out quickly Low fertility Loses soluble nutrients too readily	Add humus-forming organic matter liberally; with winter manuring, summer mulching Cultivate topsoil, well ahead of growing season Correct acidity with ground chalk Use a seaweed soil-conditioner annually
Silt	Feels silky when rubbed between finger and thumb Does not mould when squeezed	Fairly easy to work More fertile than sand	Lacks structure Feels leaden Apt to cake at surface Dries out too readily	Work in humus-forming organic matter liberally Top-dress with clay or clay-marl in winter Correct acidity with chalk or fine limestone dust Improve conditions with gypsum or powdered seaweed
Loams	Blends of sand and clay mainly Retains shape when compressed Smears the skin when rubbed Slightly gritty if a light loam Polishes and leave heavy smearing if a heavy loam	Moisture-retentive Crumb structure Inherently fertile Good to work		Respond readily to humus-forming organic matter, worked into the topsoil in autumn-winter Lime lightly to correct any acidity Otherwise, the best of soils for gardening
Clay	Feels sticky and plastic Retains shape when moulded Leaves heavy smears on fingers	Inherently fertile Amenable to change	Heavy to work Dense, slow to warm up Waterlogs easily Cakes and cracks on drying out	Add gypsum to improve porosity in autumn/winter Add lime in any form in offsetting acidity Expose soil to weathering by rough deep digging or ridging in autumn Incorporate humus-forming organic matter liberally

A Quick Guide to Soils—Continued

Type of soil	Identifiable characteristics	Good points	Bad points	Treatments needed for Improvement
Calcareous (Chalk, Limy)	Whitish sub-surface soil, often with chalky or limestone lumps	Adaptable for many lime-tolerant ornamental plants	Excess alkalinity Poor fertility, hungry for organic matter Needs good management	Break up in depth without bringing fragments upwards, thereafter cultivate topsoil only Add humus-forming organic matter freely, especially peat, pulverised bark, strong manures, and mulches Give balanced fertilizers, acid-reacting Sulphur, aluminium and ferrous sulphates, used judiciously, offset high alkalinity
Peat (Fen)	Rich brown to black colour Spongy, fibrous nature, moist	Easy to work Ideal for lime-intolerant plants	Over-acid Often ill-drained Apt to shrink in cultivation	Increase drainage, where water table is high Add ground limestone or chalk to reduce acidity Dress a sandy or silty light peat with marl Add actively decomposing organic matter Basic slag, bone meal, nitro-chalk are useful fertilizers

lime and is neutral or only slightly acid overall.

Too little lime not only denies plants the essential calcium as a nutrient but allows other elements of a toxic nature to become more freely available. Too much lime can also adversely affect many plants, and some soils, derived largely from chalk or limestone rocks, need cultivations that will increase acid reactions. It is, however, easier to counter soil acidity than alkalinity.

With this background knowledge, it is now possible to assess your type of soil, identify its good and bad characteristics, and plan its improvement, for few garden soils are anywhere near perfect.

Types of Soil

It is important to know your type of soil by broad definition in order to cultivate it correctly. The accompanying chart indicates the usual classifications, the characteristics by which they can be identified, their good and bad points, and treatments needed for their improvement.

Soil forms at the surface under the action of weathering forces, the additions of organic materials and their subsequent mixing. Fertility is greatest at the surface, but extends downwards as the various components of the soil become more mixed and integrated. Somewhat arbitrarily the more fertile surface layer is termed the topsoil and beneath its depth is the subsoil, though there is no sharp demarcation.

A soil is brought into cultivation by breaking up the topsoil by digging, ploughing or rotavating. This admits air, increases drainage, excites biochemical activity and releases fertility. It prepares the soil for sowing and planting. It enables us to make additions to the soil, such as organic matter, lime and fertilizers, for its amendment and enrichment. Usually, cultivations are confined to the topsoil, sometimes referred to as the top-spit—a spit being the depth to which a spade blade is used.

Subsoil and Drainage

Subsoil begins where the soil colour becomes lighter from an increasing lack of organic matter and is more mineral in nature. It is less fertile than the topsoil, and less aerated. It receives the rains percolating through the topsoil, and these accumulate to saturation point and find a level known as the water table. This fluctuates according to rainfall and the ease with which water can move and drain away through the subsoil to springs, streams and rivers.

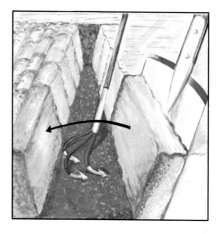

Plant roots grow downward, but can only anchor themselves well in the subsoil and take moisture from it, if it is sufficiently porous and well-drained to avoid saturation, stagnation and a water table that does not persist either high or long. Good drainage at subsoil level is vital to plant health and vigour. A simple check is to make a hole 60cm/24in deep at the low point of your ground, and watch the water table in the hole after heavy rain. If little or no water drains in, there is good subsoil drainage. If the water level rises and sinks quickly below topsoil level, it is still satisfactory. If the water level rises high and drains only slowly, then provision for subsoil drainage should be made.

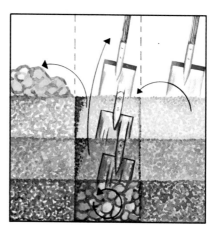

Digging

It is sensible and beneficial to prepare ground for gardening by digging with a sharp spade, kept free of clogging soil by periodic scraping, though a flat-tined fork is lighter and easier to use on sticky heavy soil. It not only admits air and light, helps drainage, and stimulates fertility, but gives the chance to remove perennial weed roots, to incorporate amendments and give a pleasing finish to the surface.

Timing is of some importance. It is desirable to give the soil time to reconsolidate before the

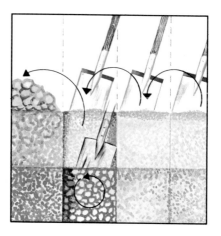

A series showing digging to two spades' depth. Note where each spadeful of soil is put

growing season, and subject to conditions being favourable – not too dry and hard, not too wet – digging is best done at least a few weeks before sowing or planting time, in autumn or winter; though light soils can be left longer than heavy.

Simple or plain digging, which means turning and breaking up the topsoil one spit, or spade blade deep, is sufficient for soils already in cultivation or which have good porous and free-draining subsoils. Take out a trench 30cm/12in wide and a spit deep; transfer this soil to the other end of the area to be dug, or, if large, mark out in two equal parallel areas, transfer the soil of the trench from one half to the opposite end of the other half, and work up one half and down the other, so that the excavated soil fills in the last trench of the adjacent half.

Turn the soil in strips or rows, inverting to bury any annual weeds. Organic matter can be strewn along the base of the trench as the soil is turned, or over the surface first and then turned in with the soil.

Where the soil is on the heavy side, and where the subsoil has been noted to be hard and relatively impervious, it is best to dig deeper by the system known as bastard trenching. The first trench is taken out 60cm/24in wide, and the soil placed aside to fill in the last trench. This gives room to break up the exposed subsoil a spit deep with a fork, or if chalky or stony with a pick-axe or mattock. This subsoil is left in situ. It can usefully be dressed with amend-ments – limestone dust and grit if acidic; gypsum if very dense; or chopped turf or fibrous organic matter if very barren.

It is doubtful that full trenching which entails disturbing the soil to three spits deep is really rewarding save for special features such as permanent asparagus beds, borders, or sweet peas on stiff heavy soils. As an alternative to simple digging on a sticky heavy clay, soil can be ridged. The ground is worked in 75–90cm/30–36in wide strips; the middle spadeful is turned forward, and then the left and right hand spadefuls are turned on top to form a ridge. No attempt is made to break the clods

down. Let exposed to the weather and the action of frost and thaw, the ridges are broken down to a workable tilth in spring.

Compost Making

Digging in itself will eventually lead to an impoverished, worn-out soil. The greatest soil-builder – except possibly on peat – is humus formed from organic matter. This can be incorporated with digging or used for mulching or topdressing soil occupied by plants. Such materials as animal manures, poultry litter, peat, leaf-mould, pulverized bark, spent hops, spent mushroom compost, weathered sawdust, shoddy, seaweed, and the prepared proprietary products are all eligible and good humus-formers. A further invaluable source is compost made from the plant waste and debris, lawn mowings, leaves and organic kitchen waste regularly available from garden and home.

As it becomes available such material is heaped in layers of 10–15cm/4–6in thick, nicely moist but not saturated, dressed with an activator or accelerator of decomposition (QR, Garotta, Bio, Comprot are proprietary activators, or thin layers of fresh animal manure or nitrogenous fertilizer such as nitro-chalk), a sprinkling of topsoil and possibly a dusting of lime; repeated until the heap is complete. Compost is best made in a container – a simple bin of wooden slats, openwork brickwork or stones, 90–120cm/36–48in square, and at least 120cm/48in high; a semi-rigid plastic round bin with aeration holes in the sides; or even an open-ended cylinder of PVC, polythene or large empty plastic bag, punched with small holes in the walls, and arranged on wood stakes or a circle of pig-netting for supports.

Coarse and fine materials should be mixed when possible. Moisture-rich materials such as lawn mowings are best wilted for a day or two before being added. A cover against the rain and weather is essential to prevent over-wetting or cooling, by tented sheet polythene or corrugated sheeting. The material soon heats up as it decomposes under bacterial and chemical attack, and shrinks in bulk. It can be turned top

Above: howing between rows
Right: straw for composting

to bottom, sides to middle, to quicken decomposition further; or simply left until a crumbly, brownish, sweet earthy-scented mould that can be easily applied to the soil, in 12–16 weeks.

Liming

The need for lime arises on most cultivated soils from time to time. Lime is needed to counteract the natural tendency for soils to become more acid, and ensure the maximum availability of nutrients in the soil solution to plants. It provides calcium, an essential plant nutrient; and most garden plants grow best in soils containing some free lime. Its presence encourages beneficial soil micro-organisms and earthworms, but discourages soil-borne diseases and pests. It improves solid structure by flocculating clay particles into small granules, with benefit to aeration and drainage.

The need for lime is best ascertained by topsoil testing, either with litmus test paper or an indicator fluid that shows the degree of acidity by its colour reaction (PBI, Sudbury, and BDH Lime Testers are brands of Soil Testers for Lime).

When lime is needed, it is best applied in winter, after digging and organically manuring the soil, strewn evenly over the surface to be weathered in. Ground chalk or limestone remain active for 2–4 years; hydrated powder lime acts more quickly and may be applied in smaller amount.

Sowing and Planting

By late winter or early spring, the prepared soil is ready to be lightly forked and raked to a fine crumblike tilth in a spell of fine weather when it is just beginning to dry. This is the time to apply fertilizers, designed to provide plants with essential nutrients for their sustenance and growth. Such fertilizers should be compounded to provide plants with a balance of the major nutrients they need, according to their kind; especially nitrogen for stem and leaf growth, phosphorus for root activity, flower and fruit formation and good ripening of growth, potash for healthy growth, disease resistance and

27

Taking out a drill with the handle of a rake

Always label every row

Tap the seeds out of the packet for even sowing

colour in flowers and fruits. The appropriate or recommended amount should be raked in some days prior to sowing or planting.

Seeds need only moisture, air and warmth to germinate, but the most influential factor is soil temperature. Seeds in cold wet soil are slow to germinate and often rot. It is wise to wait until soil temperatures run at 15–18°C/60–65°F before sowing most seeds out of doors. The old adage has it 'Sow dry, transplant wet'. Once seeds are rooting they seek nutrients from the soil; and seedlings are ready for transplanting as soon as they are making true plant leaves. They transplant best when young, and make good progress if they can then be set in soil nicely moist, and with their seed leaves at soil level.

5 The Lawn

Getting the Site Ready

Clearing

This is a task which *must* be carried out thoroughly because a lawn is a permanent feature in a garden and poor 'workmanship' cannot be rectified easily later on. Sites will vary considerably from the virgin ground of new property, to a badly neglected site which is overgrown with weeds.

The first job is to examine the area and remove all debris in the form of large stones and bricks. On new sites quite a lot of builders' rubbish is left behind and some of this can be used later on for the base of paths or foundations for a garage or even a greenhouse.

Where the site is overgrown, the weeds must be cut down and the growth placed on a compost heap. Do not place perennial weeds on the heap as these can take root again! These weeds must be dug out without breaking their roots off. Put them aside in a neat heap and then burn them later when dry on a bonfire. If possible, the lawn site should be prepared well in advance of lawn-making and a period three or four months beforehand is ideal.

Digging

Once cleared, the area should be cultivated to the full depth of the spade or fork. On a new site some of the good or better quality topsoil may have been buried by the builders and this should be 'rescued' by burying the poorer quality subsoil below the rest of the digging as work proceeds. Always keep the good soil at the top of the work.

If the soil is heavy or sticky, it should be opened up or lightened by the inclusion of sharp sand or well-weathered cinders. All soils must be fed with as much organic matter as possible and this can take the form of horticultural peat, composted vegetable waste or well-rotted farm-yard manure if you are fortunate enough to acquire some. This organic matter will encourage a vigorous root action as the grass becomes established and will also act as a 'sponge' and retain moisture. This is especially important where soils are light. These tend to dry out quickly in hot weather.

About one bucketful of compost, peat or old manure should be applied per square yard of ground. All material must be thoroughly mixed in with the top 25–30cm/10–12in of soil.

When the site has been dug or forked over it is a good plan to allow the soil to settle for at least 3–4 weeks before any further work is carried out. If this period can be extended to two months so much the better.

When is the best time to cultivate the site? Preferably in the late autumn if the soil is heavy so that it can overwinter and be broken down by winter and early spring frosts. Lighter soils can be cultivated at most periods of the year.

Levelling

Many gardeners seem to think that a lawn must be perfectly level. This is true if you want to play bowls! To facilitate mowing, the site should be reasonably level so that the mower does not scalp the surface in uneven areas. Ideally, a slight slope away from the house is ideal so that the site drains well.

Sites will vary, of course, and in some cases quite a lot of levelling may be required–bringing soil from high areas to the low ones. Try to work with the contours to minimize labour. On a very steep slope, for example, it may be wise to arrange the lawn feature in two distinct levels.

Levelling is quite a simple operation. Determine the level to which you want to work, bearing the previous remarks in mind. Drive in a wooden peg at this level and then drive in further pegs spaced about 2m/6ft apart over the site. These other pegs are levelled to the level of the first peg by laying a straight-edged plank across and checking the level with a spirit level placed on the edge of the plank and approximately at its centre. The pegs should be driven into the ground until a true level reading is obtained.

The soil is then raked about, adding or drawing some away until the surface of the soil is level with the tops of all the pegs. In some cases, it may well be necessary to bring in some extra quality topsoil when the site is very uneven or the depth of good soil all over the selected site is of poor quality generally. During levelling operations, care must be taken to see that poorer subsoil is never brought to the surface.

Final Tilth or Surface
If the preparations of the site are undertaken during the spring, summer or autumn months, some weed growth will occur before the lawn is finally made if several weeks are allowed to elapse before seed is sown or turf is laid. Occasional light hoeing of the surface, especially during warm weather or drying winds, will kill off most weed seedlings.

A fine surface is important, especially if grass seed is to be sown, so thorough breaking down of the lumpy surface is necessary. The back of the fork will break up lumps easily, but generally,

A well-kept lawn is essential to the overall appearance of any garden

the garden rake will be adequate. Cross-raking will eventually produce a fine tilth and as the work proceeds, all stones should be removed.

A general or balanced fertilizer can be applied at this stage (10–14 days before sowing seed or turfing) and 55–85g per sq m/2–3oz per sq yd should be adequate. If the soil is light, it is a good idea to tread over the area so that the soil is consolidated or settled. Afterwards a raking over will level off the site.

Try to select dry weather for this final surface preparation. The soil will break up better and treading on the site will not compact the soil too much.

A Lawn from Seed

There is no doubt that the best quality lawns are those which are made by sowing grass seed. Great strides have been made in the development of grass seed mixtures and now it is possible to purchase special blends for particular purposes such as heavy soils, shade, hard wear, and so on. Most of the lawns made from seed have a hard-wearing mixture in them so that they can withstand the tough conditions of family usage–especially where children are concerned! It should be appreciated that the finer, choicer grasses will not withstand hard usage and they are more suited to the ornamental features where a really beautiful velvet-like finish is desired. They are also demanding on care and attention.

A lawn raised from seed is not the 'instant' lawn the one made from turves would be. Quick though many of the modern seeds are to germinate and become reasonably well-established, several weeks must elapse from sowing date before they can be enjoyed.

One can make up an excellent blend oneself if the following types of seed are used–20 per cent browntop bent and 80 per cent Chewing's fescue. This mix will produce a good-looking and hard-wearing lawn. However, most good garden shops or garden centres stock a useful range of pre-packed grass seed mixtures for many circumstances.

How to Sow

The best times to sow grass seed are either in April or August or September. The latter date is suitable for the warmer parts of the country. The rate of application is 45g per sq m/1½oz per sq yd for the general-purpose or hard-wearing seed mixtures, and 28g per sq m/1oz per sq yd for the finer grasses.

Sowing must be as even as possible and to facilitate this, it is a good idea to mark out the area with strips. Each strip should be 1m/3ft wide and two lines can be used for this purpose. Two canes placed across the lines and spaced 30cm/12in apart will mark out each sq m/sq yd to be sown. A cane is moved 30cm/12in forward each time as work proceeds. With a little experience or practice, these canes can be dispensed with and the amount per sq m/sq yd judged simply with the aid of the two lines. These are moved across the site as the sowing progresses.

Take your time during the sowing operation, making quite sure that very even coverage of the ground is carried out. Avoid working during windy weather as the seed will be blown about badly.

After an area has been sown, the seed should be covered in lightly by cross-raking with the garden rake. Rake in one direction first, then at right angles to this with the second raking. Only allow the rake's teeth to bite into the fine topsoil by about 1cm/½in.

Do not sow an area greater than the reach of your rake before the covering operation is undertaken. You must not tread about on sown ground. Most of the grass seed sold today is treated with bird repellant, but if birds are persistent in thieving the seed, you must place a criss-cross pattern of black thread over the area to discourage them.

Watering

Keep a close eye on weather conditions after the seed has been sown and if prolonged periods of dry or warm weather persist, it may be necessary to water the site–especially if the soil is on the light side and tends to dry out rapidly. Use a

Lawns are difficult to maintain
around a tree, but the effort can be
worthwhile

sprinkler with a fine distribution of water or one of the special irrigation hoses which emit a mist of water gently over the ground. This type of watering really soaks into the soil.

The First Cut

The young grass must not be cut too soon and about six to seven weeks will elapse approximately before the blades of grass are about two inches long and ready for their first cut. Before this, though, it is a good idea to firm the young grass roots in by a *light* rolling. Running over the area with the rear roller of the lawnmower is usually sufficient.

Just before the first cut is made, go over the site and remove any small stones etc–a very light brushing will help. Set the mower's blades high–about 2.5cm/1in. This just 'tops' the foliage and encourages the grass to thicken up. Later mowings are carried out with the mower's blades set progressively lower–1.8cm/¾in to a final 1cm/½in or so. This latter setting will be the one which the grass is cut to for the rest of the mowing season.

It is most important that the mower's blades are nice and sharp for these first cuts. Do not mow when the grass is damp or wet–this will cause the blades to rip out a lot of the tender grass.

A Lawn from Turf

For the impatient gardener, a lawn constructed from turf is the ideal solution. Within a few days of laying, the area can be used and enjoyed and the 'instant' green effect is especially welcome if you are creating a garden from scratch.

The most favourable period for the laying of turves is much greater than that for grass seed. Late February to late September is the period, but it is unwise to attempt the work during very dry weather in the summer. If one is allowed to use the hose-pipe in summer, then the hot, dry weather need not be quite such a problem.

It is, however, better to work in the cooler, wetter periods so that there is less time and labour involved in artificial watering. The individual turves will also knit together more quickly.

Turf is usually obtained from local sources and nurseries can often supply. Addresses of suppliers can also be obtained from advertisements in the local evening and weekend newspapers. Garden shops often have addresses of local suppliers too. It is difficult to control the quality of turf and it can vary considerably from supplier to supplier. Quite often local gardeners can recommend a particular supplier of good quality turf.

Most good suppliers prepare their turf sources by pre-weeding and spiking or aeration. With some care and attention to the use of selective weedkillers and lawn feeds, even quite poor quality turf can, in a few seasons, be brought back to a reasonable appearance. It does pay, however, to scout around a little to discover a supplier of the better quality turf. Turf is usually supplied in individual pieces, each being 30×90cm/12×36in–a metre/yard of turf.

Calculating Requirements
This is an easy exercise. Measure the length and width of the site. Divide the width by 3 and then multiply this number by the total *length* of the site. This will give the total number of whole turves required. For example–a site is 36ft wide and 20ft long. Divide the width by 3 which gives a figure of 12. Multiply this figure by the total length which is 20, and the total number of turves required to cover this site will be 240.

Your turves will be delivered on the verge outside your home and you must be ready to get them into your garden as quickly as possible so that they are not an obstruction and to prevent them decomposing if left in their stack. Few delivery lorries (they are very heavy when loaded!) will drive over cross-overs in case of damage.

Laying Turf
Commence by laying whole turves across the width of the site. If necessary cut the end turf to fit the site. Be careful not to use a very narrow piece on the edge. It is better to cut to size, then use a whole piece placed to the edge of the site and then put this trimmed piece inside next to it.

An alternative solution is to lay whole turves down the length of the site on the edges, and then fill in across the site with whole turves, cutting the last ones in each row to fit inside the edging turves.

As turves are laid, make sure that the soil is raked level and is firmed. It may be necessary to push or take away some soil occasionally if some of the turves have not been cut evenly in thickness. This is where it really pays to obtain quality turf. All the turves must be bonded like bricks in a wall. This means that vertical joints in one row do not fall directly opposite those in the previous row. To cause this stagger in joints, the first turf of every other row should be cut in half and laid. The remaining turves in that row will be *whole* turves. This cutting will be necessary when whole turves are laid down the length of a site at the edges as mentioned earlier.

As each row is laid, a little fine soil, mixed with some moist peat, should be worked with the

Above left: turves will give an instant lawn
Below left: a games lawn must be made from hard-wearing grasses
Above right: in a small garden, a circular lawn is often effective
Below right: if you set paving stones in grass, make sure the mower will clear them

joints. This will help the turves to knit together quickly and will prevent drying out and curling of the edges in dry weather.

Work from a plank placed on the first row of turves and work forward down the site, moving the plank forward into the row of turves just laid down. In this way you avoid treading on the prepared site. As each turf is laid, make sure that it is butted up firmly against the other turves. A home-made tamping block can be used to beat the turf lightly down as the work proceeds.

When the site has been turfed, roll the grass with a light roller or use the rear roller of the mower. To give more weight, a few bricks can be carefully placed on the mower. Roll across the lawn and then down its length.

A half-moon edging iron will be a useful piece

Above: the lawn will benefit from sprinkling in dry weather
Left: small electric trimmers are available for lawn edges

of equipment when it is necessary to cut the turves to any desired shape at the edges. Curves are easily cut out and if an irregular outline to flower borders is required, a length of hose-pipe can be laid out on the grass to the desired shapes and the turves cut out with this tool.

After Care
The main requirement may be to keep the turf watered if dry weather prevails. Drying winds can cause problems too, so a watchful eye must be maintained. It will be necessary to examine all the bonds and add some fine soil and peat where necessary. Replace any sections of turf which have failed to 'take'. Quite often, this is caused by poor contact with the prepared soil beneath, so make sure that replacement pieces are pressed firmly in place.

Autumn-laid turf will not grow very much, but will be ready for its first cut in the spring of the following year. Set the mower's blades high for the first few cuts and then lower them gradually.

Routine Management
The main task will be the cutting of the grass. The period for this will depend to a great extent on the weather conditions, the type of soil on which the grass is grown, and of course, on the location of the garden. Generally speaking, the cutting season starts in March and continues until October and sometimes into November.

How often should one mow the lawn? Usually, at least once a week, but it may be necessary to cut twice a week if the grass is growing vigorously. The grass should not be cut too closely and a 1cm/½in cut is adequate. When a lawn is used heavily, it is wise to allow a little more grass to remain and a cut to 2.5cm/1in is advisable.

Do check over the lawn before mowing to remove stones and other debris which could damage the mower's blades. When selecting a new mower, remember that a cylinder type of cut will provide a finer and better finish. A rotary mower will cut long, tough grass as well as ordinary grass, but the finish is not quite as good as the cylinder mower. Grass collection is useful too, although leaving some cuttings on the surface is helpful as a mulch or top-dressing in dry weather. It reduces the drying out of the surface soil.

Where allowed to do so in dry periods, artificial watering should be given frequently to keep the grass growing well. In autumn and early spring give the lawn a thorough raking or scarifying with a special lawn rake. This action will remove the 'thatch' or debris which collects or mats the surface. This will allow the roots to 'breath' more efficiently. Aeration or spiking with the garden fork or a special lawn aerator will make drainage holes in the soil surface a few inches deep. This should be undertaken in early autumn and/or early spring.

A lawn needs feeding. Specially formulated,

easy to use lawn fertilizers are available. Usually, a feed is given in the autumn and again in the spring. The former feed stimulates root growth ready for the following season. The latter encourages that lovely green growth of the foliage. On large lawn areas, the use of a fertilizer spreader saves a lot of time and effort. Make sure that autumn leaves are removed regularly from the lawn. Special leaf sweepers are available which are a great aid on the larger lawn areas.

Weed Control

Keeping the lawn free from weeds is a much easier task these days, thanks to the introduction of selective weedkillers which seek out the weeds, destroy them and allow the grass to grow without harm. There are even combined lawn feeds and weedkillers so that you can feed and weed in one operation.

The grass should not be mown for at least four days after the use of weedkillers. The most effective time to use selectives is from May to July. Weedkillers are best applied in damp weather—never during hot, dry conditions.

To kill moss—a very common trouble—use a special lawn-sand or a proprietary moss-killing preparation. This is applied in the spring or early summer. Dead matter can be removed by a thorough raking about three to four weeks after treatment.

Where selective weedkillers are used it is necessary to give the grass a 'tonic' about two weeks beforehand. This is a fertilizer dressing which strengthens the grass ready for the action of the weedkiller.

6 Annuals and Biennials

Annuals are the 'decoration' of a garden – the embroidery on a plainer background. They are gay and impermanent, making patches of colour for a few weeks and then fading. For the most part they are undemanding and will grow in any sort of soil. They can be scattered haphazardly and left to fend for themselves or they can be carefully thinned out and propped up with low brushwood when they will make quite large plants with more showy heads. Sometimes, if they have flowered early during a good summer they will seed themselves and if the seedlings stand the winter you will get big plants which will flower early. Annuals fill in the gaps left by bulbs or the patches in the front of the border that are not yet filled or are left especially for them.

There are hardy annuals and half hardy annuals. The former can also be sown at any time from the middle of March until early June. It's better to choose a time when the weather is 'gentle'. Too wet and too cold soil will not help germination and sowing in a strong wind only results in the seeds blowing all over the place. Pick a comparatively mild day when the sun has warmed the soil a little and rake the soil in the chosen place to as fine a tilth as possible. Brush the top 1cm/½in of soil to one side with your hand and flatten it very gently, then scatter the seeds as thinly as possible and either brush the topsoil back or sprinkle peat or sifted soil over them to the depth of about ½cm/¼in. Put in a label to show where they are and if you have a cat cover them with some wire netting. Cats are idle creatures and a patch of soil that is easily scratched over saves them a lot of trouble. According to the time of year and the weather the seeds will take 2–4 weeks to germinate. When they are big enough to handle thin them out according to the instructions on the packet. This can be a tedious job but is well worth while. Some seeds are very minute and it is extremely difficult to sow them thinly. Others are big enough to be put in place. The instructions on the packet usually say how far apart they should be and how high they should grow.

You cannot really do anything with the seeds you thin out. Just occasionally if it's a mild, damp day they will transplant if put immediately into a hole made with a small stick but even then they will need watching and watering and unless you have a lot of time and enthusiasm this is not worthwhile. Concentrate on those that are left and as they get bigger put short, brushy twigs all over the area. Although they should make plants strong enough to stand alone, a summer storm soon flattens them.

Half-hardy annuals are those which have to be sown in seed boxes or tiny pots and only put outdoors when all danger of frost is past. This can mean pricking them off from the seed box into another box so that they make plants large enough to handle when it is time to put them outside. A greenhouse is the ideal place to start growing them but a sunny window sill or anywhere that gets good light and is frost free will do. If all that is too much bother boxes of pricked out half-hardy annuals can be bought.

Biennials are the plants that are sown in early summer of one year, planted into the position in which they are required to grow that autumn and they will flower the next summer. Their

Candytuft – one of the best-loved annuals

cultivation requires a specially set aside space in which to sow the seeds and in a small garden this may be difficult. As with the half-hardy annuals one can buy boxes or plants of biennials which can be put straight into their flowering position. It's really a question of whether you would rather pay for someone else's time and labour or do it yourself for the price of a packet of seeds.

List of Popular Annuals

Annual Coreopsis *(Calliopsis)*
These have attractive golden yellow daisy like flowers with brown centres. They grow to about 60cm/24in and are very good for cutting. There is also a dwarf variety with flowers of crimson,

gold and maroon. These will tolerate difficult conditions and are good in town gardens.

California Poppy *(Eschscholzia)*
Another tongue twister of a name for a delightful old-fashioned flower sometimes known as Granny's Nightcap. It will grow on poor, dry soil and likes full sunlight when it will produce flowers that are double, semi-double and single in lovely shades of red, pink, orange, yellow and white and are about 30cm/12in high.

Candytuft
A delightful, cottage garden type annual that comes in white or shades of mauve and pink. It will grow, in almost any soil or situation, to a height of 23–38cm/9–15in.

Clarkia

These have long spikes of double flowers in shades of pink, purple, carmine and white. They reach a height of 60cm/24in and are graceful and easily grown. They will look better if the clumps are not too big.

Cornflower

A splendid flower for cutting and one that likes sunshine and any kind of soil. One thinks of cornflowers as being blue but they also come in bright rose and in mixed shades of blue, pink and rose. They reach a height of 60–90cm/24–36in.

Godetia

These are easy to grow, colourful and long lasting. They like sunshine and come in shades of pink, mauve and salmon. They make plants of 30-45cm/12–18in.

Larkspur

This is an old-fashioned flower associated with cottage gardens but the modern varieties are large and have beautiful violet, rose, salmon and white flowers that are delphinium-like. They grow to 90–120cm/36–48in.

Limnanthes

This delightful little flower is like fried eggs. It grows to only 15cm/6in and has yellow, saucer-shaped blossoms edged with white and the bees love it. It is easily grown and frequently seeds itself.

Love-in-a-Mist (Nigella)

An old favourite and one of the prettiest of annuals. The most usual variety is blue but there is a mixture of jewel shades of blue, rose and white. The flowers hide amidst delicate feathery foliage and the seed pod is as decorative as the flower. They grow 38–45cm/15–18in tall.

Love-Lies-Bleeding (Amaranthus caudatus)

These are not so showy as some annuals but are

Godetia lasts well

Love-in-a-mist, an old favourite

Nasturtiums grow well in very poor soil

interesting as cut flowers. They grow about 75cm/30in and have long drooping tassels of flowers in either deep crimson or greenish yellow.

Mallow *(Lavatera)*
This annual makes a bushy plant 90–120cm/ 36–48in tall and is good at the back of a border. The flowers are pink and it blooms from August until well into the Autumn.

Marigold *(Calendula)*
Very easy to grow, sturdy and gay. Calendulas come in all shades of yellow and orange. They need a minimum of attention and can be bought in individual colours or in mixed shades. They grow from 45–60cm/18–24in tall.

Mignonette
Another annual renowned for its fragrance. The flowers are spikes of pale green or dull red and are by no means showy and the seeds do not always germinate well but it is well worth growing for its scent.

Nasturtium
These gay yellow, orange, salmon, scarlet and primrose flowers will bring colour to the dryest place. There are dwarf ones, bushy ones that form runners and are splendid in hanging

Cut off any dead poppy heads to encourage further flowering

Poppies

Poppies come in many annual varieties. All are easy and produce lots of lovely flowers. The only difficulty is that the seed is so fine that it is almost impossible to sow it thinly and a lot of thinning out is necessary. They range from 75–105cm/30–42in tall in all shades of pink.

Saponaria

This makes a very pretty flower for cutting. It grows easily and the graceful sprays of pink flowers reach a height of 45–60cm/18–24in.

Star of the Veldt (Dimorphotheca)

A difficult name but a lovely daisy like flower that rejoices in sunshine. The flowers range from bluish white through lemon, golden yellow and orange to salmon orange and grow to only 23–30cm/9–12in so are ideal for the front of a border.

Sunflower

A very decorative flower that will last well into the autumn. The big yellow flowers grow from 120–240cm/4–8ft tall.

List of Half-Hardy Annuals

Annual Pinks (Dianthus)

These sweetly scented little flowers may be treated as annuals and sown outdoors from April onwards, but for early flowering sow them under glass and plant them out in late May. They grow about 20–30cm/8–12in high and make an excellent edging plant.

Asters

For late summer flowering asters are ideal. Their richly coloured flowers come in late August and September and bring fresh colour to rather tired gardens. There are many varieties to choose from, double and single and they vary in height from 45–75cm/18–30in.

Marigolds (French and African)

French marigolds make low plants up to 30cm/12in high with brilliant flowers in shades of yellow, orange and mahogany red.

African marigolds bear enormous double

baskets and tall ones that will climb up walls and trellises.

Night-scented Stock (Matthiola bicornis)

These unobtrusive little flowers of lilac mauve grow about 30cm/12in high and spend the day looking shrivelled and half dead but in the evening they open up and have a wonderful fragrance. Grow them under a window or round a terrace so that you can enjoy the scent on warm summer evenings.

Pincushion Flower (Scabious)

These can be treated as half-hardy annuals but outdoor sowings will produce flowers from August until the frost comes. The flowers are excellent for cutting and come in shades of pink, cerise, crimson, lavender, dark maroon and white and are about 60cm/24in tall.

flowers on strong, bushy plants. The colours are wonderfully vivid, yellow, orange and dark red and the flowers are long lasting. They grow from 45–60cm/18–24in tall.

Mesembryanthemum
If you've a dry and sunny spot this is a wonderful plant. Only 1cm/3in high the brilliant, daisy like flowers come in pink, carmine, salmon, apricot and orange.

Morning Glory (Ipomoea)
This very beautiful flower grows well in a pot in a cold greenhouse or against a sunny wall. The seedling doesn't like being handled so it is really best to sow one or two in a pot and put the pot against a wall or fence outside. Place it facing the morning sun and at breakfast time you will be greeted by convolvulus-type flowers of the most wonderful blue.

Nemesia
Another brilliant flower for the front of the border. It grows 23–30cm/9–12in high and is quick flowering.

Nicotiana (Flowering Tobacco)
These are subdued flowers that grow from 30–45cm/12–24in high. The paler ones are usually the most fragrant and some varieties are sold as being sweetly scented, especially at night. There is a particularly lovely lime green variety that is very popular with flower arrangers.

Petunias
Petunias are excellent flowers for window boxes, tubs and bedding, especially in dry weather. There is a great variety of colour in all shades of pink, mauve and red and some very beautiful white ones. They make spreading but reasonably compact plants that vary from 30–45cm/12–18in in height.

Phlox Drummondii
A delightful gay little flower with a maximum height of 2cm/5in with blooms of pink, rose, salmon, crimson, scarlet and violet blue.

Salvia
If red is your colour this is the flower for you. Its brilliant scarlet spikes of bloom grow 30–38cm/12–15in tall. There are a few more subdued varieties but the scarlet is the most popular.

Snapdragon (Antirrhinum)
These well-known and very popular flowers come in all colours of yellow, orange, red and white and there is a hybrid variety with butterfly like blooms which grows up to 1m/36in tall. Others range from dwarf varieties of 20–30cm/8–12in to the more usual kinds that reach from 45–60cm/18–24in.

Stocks
These beautifully scented flowers are lovely in any garden. The ten week variety or the ordinary stock are those to pick for summer flowering and they come in shades of blood-red, rose pink, lavender, cream and white and reach a height of 30–60cm/12–24in.

Strawflower (Helichrysum)
An 'everlasting' flower with stiff, crackly paper-like petals that is very attractive and easy to grow. It comes in rose, crimson, orange, and white and plants are from 30–75cm/18–30in tall.

Sweet Pea
Sweet peas may be sown outdoors from March until May or in pots or boxes in a greenhouse or frame during January and February and planted out in April after they have been hardened off. They can also be sown in pots or boxes in September and October and wintered in a cold frame. The tall varieties can reach 2m/6ft and will need netting, canes or some other form of support, but there are shorter varieties.

Tagetes
This is a gay little plant suitable for edging a border. The flowers come in yellow, orange and mahogany red, like tiny French marigolds, and they only grow 15–25cm/6–10in high.

Verbena
A richly colourful plant that doesn't grow more than 30cm/12in high and will thrive even in wet weather. It's bright flowers may be violet, coral pink, salmon or scarlet.

Zinnias

Splendid flowers that come in beautiful colours but they don't like being disturbed, so it is often better to sow them where they are to flower but wait until May or June when the soil is warm. They vary in height from dwarf varieties at 10–15cm/4–6in to those that attain 60–75cm/24–30in.

Canterbury bells

Foxgloves will grow well in shade

List of Biennials

Campanula

These pretty bell-like plants come in shades of blue, lavender and white. There are dwarf varieties for edging or rock gardens; trailing varieties for hanging baskets or window boxes and tall varieties that can grow from 60–120cm/24–48in tall.

Canterbury Bell

A much-loved, old-fashioned flower with single or semi double bells in pink, lavender, blue and white and ranging in height from 45–75cm/18–30in. The cup and saucer variety is especially lovely.

Forget-Me-Not (Myosotis)

The blue of forget-me-not is lovely with tulips and wallflowers. They make compact little plants, 15–20cm/6–8in high and left undisturbed will seed themselves. Usually blue, there is a very pretty pink variety.

Foxglove (Digitalis)

The modern strains of foxglove produce flowers in shades of cream, pink and white, many of them beautifully spotted. They are valuable for growing in shady borders and flower in July and August on spikes from 1–2m/3–6ft high.

Honesty

These pretty mauve flowers turn to lovely silver seed pods which are very decorative and last through the winter. They reach a height of 60cm/24in.

Iceland Poppy (Papaver rudicaule)

These lovely poppies come in all shades of yellow, apricot, orange and white and grow about 45cm/18in high. They make beautiful cut flowers but their stems must be dipped into boiling water for 30 seconds or burnt over a flame. Otherwise they will not last.

Salvia Haematodes

This is a lovely relation of the red, annual salvia. It likes a light, well-drained soil and its soft mauve spikes reach a height of 90–120cm/36–48in.

Sweet Williams–an old-fashioned cottage garden flower

Wallflowers provide a splendid show of early colour

Siberian Wallflower (*Cheiranthus*)
This is a splendid plant for spring bedding. It has brilliant yellow or orange flowers that bloom from March till May and grows to a height of 38cm/15in.

Stock (Brompton)
This is a beautiful, scented biennial which will flower outdoors from March till May. If possible winter them in a cold frame or give them some protection except in very mild districts. The flowers are lavender, rose, pink and white and reach a height of 45cm/18in.

Sweet William
This is a cottage garden flower that produces sweetly scented blooms in June and July. The head of flowers is borne on a sturdy stem and comes in pink, salmon, crimson and white. There is a dwarf variety but the taller ones reach a height of 45cm/18in.

Wallflowers
These flower from March until May. There are many lovely colours, mostly cream, gold and a deep red and brown there are also pale pinks and mauves. The most strongly scented is the blood red variety which is particularly good under a south facing window. There are dwarf varieties but the most usual ones grow to about 45–60cm/18–24in.

7 Perennials

Planning and Planting a Border

The width of a border determines the height of plants which should be used. As a rough guide, half the width of the border should equal the height of the tallest plants. A good width for a border is 3–3.5m/10–12ft, with plants from 30cm/12in to 150cm/5ft tall. Planting in drifts will give a note of informality, and it is worth remembering that several plants of a kind together are more effective than the odd one dotted about.

You can design your border using graph paper, or paper ruled in squares. Mark the border itself at 3m/10ft intervals with canes to act as guides. Make sure that you have left sufficient room between the groups of plants for their eventual height and spread. Plant the tallest plants first. In a one sided border this will be at the back; otherwise some can go nearer the centre. Next plant the middle groups, and lastly those at the front. If the weather is dry and windy at planting time, do not put all the plants out where you will eventually plant them, but keep them covered until they are needed to prevent them drying out. Make sure all roots have planty of room to spread out, and water them generously if the ground is dry, and firm the soil around the plants.

Where the front border meets the lawn, allow for the ultimate growth of the front subjects so that they will not be damaged by the mower. Frosts tend to lift plants, and where this happens, they should be firmed back into the ground.

The plant lists below have been divided according to season, to facilitate choosing plants to give some interest all the year round.

Spring

Alyssum *Alyssum saxatile* 'Compactum' gives a brilliant golden display, 15cm/6in high, from April to July. It prefers sun but does quite well in part shade. The large grey green leaves last into the autumn.

Bergenia cordifolia has rounded glossy leathery leaves, with sprays of rose pink flowers to 23cm/9in in April and May. Some shade, not too dry. Good varieties: 'Ballawley', 'Evening Glow' and 'Margery Fish'.

Doronicum caucasicum (Leopard's Bane) Yellow daisy flowers to 45cm/18in above heart-shaped leaves in April and May. Good cut flowers. Sun or part shade.

Euphorbia polychroma Lime-yellow flower-like bracts in April and May, followed by 45cm/18in green bush that lasts all summer. Sun or part shade, most soils.

Iberis sempervirens Masses of white flowers during March, April and May. Neat little 23cm/9in dark green bush throughout summer. Trim after flowering. Sun or light shade, most soils.

Primula *Primula acaulis* is the common primrose. Needs moist shade. *Primula veris* is the cowslip. Does best in moist dappled shade.

Pulmonaria angustifolia (Lungwort) 'Munstead Blue' bears 23cm/9in sprays of blue flowers in early March. Spear shaped leaves. Light shade.

Lily of the valley will fill many awkward little spots

Soldanella alpina Mat of small rounded leaves with 8cm/3in stems of little lavender blue bells in March. Needs protection from slugs. Shady, well-drained soil with plenty of humus.

Summer
Acanthus mollis and *A. spinosus* Large deeply dissected glossy dark green leaves, purple white flowers, 105–120cm/3–4ft, July to September. Sun or part shade in well drained soil.

Achillea eupatorium Fine filigree foliage, tightly packed golden yellow flowers, 105–135cm/3–4½ft, July to September. Prefers sun.

Aconitum cammarum Violet blue flowers to more than 1m/3ft, July to September. Does best in moist shade. The roots are very poisonous.

Anaphalis nubigena Silvery green leaves, paper-textured white flowers to 30cm/12in July to October. Tolerates dry shade.

Anthemis rudolphiana Fine silver filigree foliage, less interesting golden yellow flowers June and July. 15cm/6in high. Front of well drained sunny border.

Armeria maritima Deep pink flowers on stems to 15cm/6in June to September. Evergreen hummock of grassy leaves. Sunny well-drained soil.

Artemisia lactiflora From 120–150cm/4–5ft. Good plant for centre of island bed, with plumes from

Aquilegia, a popular garden perennial

July to September. Sun or light shade, good soil.

Aster (Michaelmas daisy) Blue, mauve or white flowers, 38–120cm/15–36in, July to October. Sun or dappled shade.

Astilbe Mostly white, pink or red, 60–90cm/2–3ft, attractive foliage over a long period. Moist shade or dappled sunlight.

Astrantia carniolica Deep red flowers, 45–75cm/18–30in high, June to September. Bright green leaves. Moist soil.

Aubrieta 'Argentovariegata' has slow steady growth, and is suitable for small gardens, pretty silver edged variegated leaves, small single mauve flowers, suitable for front of border, June to September. Sunny well drained soil.

Brunnera macrophylla Large heart-shaped dark green leaves, small sky blue flowers on 45cm/18in stems, April to June. Light shade.

Calamintha nepetoides 30cm/12in bushes with cloud of tiny light blue flowers early July to October. Small aromatic leaves. Light shades.

Campanula 'Pritchard's Variety' grows to 90cm/36in, masses of small blue flowers June to August. *C. portenschlagiana,* grows to 15cm/6in, deep lavender blue flowers, June to November. Most soils.

Catananche caerulea Flowers freely June to September. Narrow grey green leaves, flower stems to 75cm/30in, profusion of bright blue flowers with silver calices. Sharply drained soil in full sun.

Coreopsis verticillata Finely leaved bush to 45cm/18in, profusion of golden yellow star shaped flowers July to September. Good soil in sun, but will grow in light shade.

Corydalis lutea to 23cm/9in, dainty green foliage, tiny lime yellow flowers May to October. Dappled shade.

Crocosmia masonorum Long dark leaves contrasting with 75cm/30in arching sprays of orange red flowers July and August. Well drained sunny site.

Crocosmia is rewarding and easy to grow

Cynoglossum nervosum Hairy veined leaves shaped like a hound's tongue, which gives the plant its common name. Small sky blue flowers June to August. Sun or shade, most soils.

Eryngium variifolium (Sea holly) Grows to a little over 75cm/30in. Evergreen leaves marbled with cream. Curious teasel-like head, July to September. Sharply drained sunny soil.

Gentiana septemfida The easiest and most trouble free cultivated gentian. Prostrate dark leaves, large beautiful deep blue trumpets to 10cm/4in, July to September. Light shade.

Geranium 'Johnson's Blue' has a trace of purple in saucer-like flowers, borne in profusion all summer to 40cm/16in. Light shade. *G. wallichanum,* prostrate growth, white centred blue saucer-shaped flowers July to October. Light shade.

Gypsophila paniculata An old valuable favo-

Delphiniums provide a mass of exciting summer colour

urite. Flowers to 90cm/36in from July to September, tiny white, cloud-like. Well drained soil; does best on chalk.

Helenium Easy and reliable so long as there is sufficient moisture. Flowers grow 90cm/36in to 120cm/48in, July to September, in shades of orange and red. Heavy soil, plenty of sun.

Helianthus decapetalus maximus Grows to 150cm/5ft, with single sunflowers from July to September. 'Loddon Gold' bears double flowers. Heavy soil, sun.

Heliopsis 'Golden Plume' is an easy and reliable variety, double gold flowers from July to September, reaching 105cm/42in or more. Heavy soil, plenty of moisture.

Heuchera Dainty little flowers on wiry stems above evergreen foliage. Flower stems can reach 75cm/30in, and flowers can be white, pink or scarlet, May to July. 'Bressingham Hybrids' are deservedly popular. Sun or part shade.

Ligularia przewalskii This has large deeply dissected dark green leaves, sometimes tinged with purple, reaching to between 60cm/24in and 90cm/36in. Flower stems rise to 150cm/5ft, with spires made up of many small yellow flowers. Moist soil in shade.

Linum narbonnense Grows to about 45cm/18in. Small narrow blue green leaves, masses of blue flowers from June to September. Will grow in poor soil, but it must be well drained and in full sun.

Lobelia fulgens 'Bees Flame' grows to 90cm/36in, vivid scarlet flowers above beetroot coloured leaves from July to September. Rich moist soil, full sun.

Lychnis coronaria Soft silvery leaves contrasting sharply with flowers in various shades of red from June to September. Height is from 60cm/24in to 120cm/48in. Sharply drained soil in full sun.

Lythrum Grows as a tapering bush, flowers from 105cm/42in to 150cm/60in, red pink or purple, late June until October. Any soil, sun or part shade.

Macleaya The new name for Bocconia. *M. cordifolia* grows to between 120cm/48in and 150cm/60in and requires no staking. Beautiful foliage and little ivory flowers from June to September. Any soil, sun or light shade.

Monarda Perfumed leaves, flowers and roots. All varieties grow to about 90cm/36in, with red, pink or purple flowers from July to September. Good soil, full sun, but will tolerate light shade.

Nepeta faassenii 'Six Hills' is a popular variety, with a haze of lavender blue flower over blue grey leaves, to 75cm/30in, from June to October. Any soil, sun or light shade.

Penstemon 'Garnet' is a popular variety forming a leafy bush growing to 60cm/24in, and to the same width, garnet-red tubular flowers from June to September. Well drained soil, sun or light shade.

Phlox paniculata There are very many varieties; most grow to around 90cm/36in. 'Border Gem' is violet purple; 'Starfire' bright red; 'Eventide' pale mauve; 'Mother of Pearl' white, tinged with pink. Good rich soil, dappled shade, although they also do well in full sun.

Platycodon grandiflorum mariesii Fine front-of-border plant, growing to 30cm/12in. Blue salver-shaped flowers from July to September. Well worked, well drained soil, sun.

Polygonum amplexicaule astrosanguineum Will reach 105cm/42in by late August, with deep red bottle-brush flowers from July to November if there are no severe frosts. Reasonably good soil, sun or light shade.

Potentilla recta 'Warrenii' is a very long-flowering hardy perennial. Deep green serrated leaves, buttercup flower to 60cm/24in from May to October. *P. nepalensis* 'Roxana' has red-veined orange flowers from June to September. Well drained soil in sun.

Salvia superba Grows to 90cm/36in with spikes of violet purple flowers over grey-green sage leaves. 'Lubeca' grows to 75cm/30in, and 'East Friesland' is a dwarf form at 45cm/18in. Good border soil in sun or light shade.

Santolina incana 'Nana' is usually regarded as a dwarf shrub, and this makes it suitable for smaller gardens. It reaches 30cm/12in, and has aromatic silvery filigree foliage, with dull yellow little button flowers in summer. Well drained soil in sun or light shade.

Sidalcea Staking is sometimes necessary with the taller varieties. 'Wensleydale' grows to 120cm/48in, with fine foliage and masses of rose coloured flower spikes. 'Reverend Page Roberts' has beautiful light pink flowers. Flowers reach their peak in July and August. Well drained soil in full sun, plenty of moisture.

Stachys lanata Beautiful soft downy silver grey leaves. 'Olympica' has 30cm/12in stumps of pink flowers from July to September. Grows well in poor stony soil in sun or part shade. Will never do well on heavy wet soils.

Stokesia laevis 'Blue Star' grows to 45cm/18in, with large light blue cornflowers from July to September. Well drained soil, sun.

Veronica exaltata This grows to 135cm/54in, with many spikes of light sky blue flowers from July to September. *V. spicata* 'Saraband' grows to 45cm/18in with violet blue flower spikes at the same period. *V. virginica* 'Alba' is a very tall form reaching 150cm/5ft with white flowers from late July to September. Rich soil, sun or light shade.

Chrysanthemums will repay careful cultivation

Helleborus niger the Christmas rose

Autumn/Winter

Aster *A. acris* grows to 75cm/30in, bushy growth, mauve flowers August to October; *A. amellus* grows to 75cm/30in, pink or blue, August to October; *A. novae-angliae* 'Harrington's Pink' grows to 135cm/54in, pink flowers in profusion, September and October. Among the Michaelmas daisies, there are 'Marie Ballard', light blue, 90cm/36in, 'Chequers', violet purple, 60cm/24in; 'Winston Churchill', ruby red, 60cm/24in. Good soil, needs full sun.

Chrysanthemum ulginosum Grows to 150cm/5ft. Many pure white single blooms with lime yellow centres in September and October. Good soil, sun.

Helleborus niger Its white flowers are easily spoiled by rain, but are worth trying. *H. atrorubens* has purple flowers to 45cm/18in, January and February. *H. orientalis,* the lenten rose, has flowers in shades of pink, March to April, growing to 45cm/18in.

Iris foetidissima This has pale lilac blue flowers in June, but is included in this section because of its scarlet berries in winter. It grows to 60cm/24in in dry shade.

Physalis franchetii Grows to about 60cm/24in. This is known as the Chinese lantern plant, and needs to be separated from other plants because of its rapid root spread and untidy habit of growth. The vivid orange red fruits appear in the autumn and can be dried.

Rudbeckia deamii This grows in a bushy form to just over 60cm/24in, with many yellow rayed flowers with conical black eyes. Flowers from August to October. Most soils, sun or light shade.

Vernonia crinita Grows to 150cm/60in, narrow spear shaped leaves, purple spikes of flowers in October. Most soils, full sun.

8 Bulbs for Spring and Summer

When speaking about bulbs in general terms these normally include corms (Crocus) and tubers (Begonia). Bulbs can be divided into two main groups: spring flowering bulbs which are by far the most popular and summer flowering bulbs. Basically they are of very easy culture and the majority will thrive in almost any situation where good drainage is provided. The reason for this is that while in their dormant stage during the summer months the new flower and foliage is developing in embryo form inside the bulb and when planted out in the autumn the process of development simply continues.

Bulbs are extremely versatile subjects and can be used effectively in almost every conceivable situation in the garden. They may be divided into four main groups, namely Hyacinths, Daffodils and Narcissi, Tulips and the miscellaneous section which includes such genera as Aconite, Crocus, Chionodoxa, Muscari, etc.

Spring Bulbs

Apart from garden work many of the spring flowering bulbs may also be used for forcing in the home and here a specialist catalogue should be consulted to determine the suitability of the various varieties for such culture. The basic essential requirement for growing bulbs indoors is to establish an abundant root system. This is best achieved if, after planting, the pots or bowls are placed in a shaded part of the garden and covered with 13–15cm/5–6in of weathered coal ashes or peat. This will ensure a cool and even temperature and prevent drying out of the potting medium. If ornamental bowls are used it is a good idea to protect them by wrapping in newspaper; this will become soft and the top growth of the bulbs will be able to penetrate without being damaged in any way.

Once the bowls have been transferred indoors regular watering is essential but to ensure that no water is left to stand at the bottom of the bowls, which would inevitably cause the soil to turn sour, just place them on their side for a few minutes to allow any surplus to drain away.

Many of the miscellaneous bulbs are also ideal for growing in small bowls or pans and **crocuses** are one of the first to come to mind. How often however does one see these producing large quantities of foliage but alas no flowers. The diagnosis is simple, we are just too impatient and think that by placing them in a warm room we advance the flowering time. What happens in reality is that the tender flower buds shrivel up and remain deep down in amongst the foliage. Great success can be achieved from many miscellaneous bulbs if these small bowls are placed outside after planting and covered with an inch of peat to prevent drying out. Just leave them until the buds begin to show colour and then place the bowls indoors on a cool window-sill. You will find that grown this way the flowers will attain their normal size and last for a long time. After flowering do not discard the bulbs but simply turn the whole clump out of the bowl, plant in the garden and leave until the foliage has turned yellow; the bulbs may then be lifted and re-planted at their proper depth and normal spacing in a permanent place.

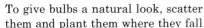

To give bulbs a natural look, scatter them and plant them where they fall

Daffodils and grape hyacinths growing in a raised bed where they can be admired from indoors on cold days

The **Narcissi** family embraces a large number of different types, ranging from the giant flowered golden harvest to its tiny miniature form minimus with numerous varieties of different sizes and colours in between, the earliest starting to bloom in February and the latest to continue into May. Most varieties are ideal for naturalizing but when planting for this purpose the major points to observe are early planting, September being the ideal month, and depth of planting. Except for the miniatures, where a depth of 5–8cm/2–3in is sufficient, the large flowered ones should have 13–15cm/5–6in of soil on top of the bulbs. This will ensure that after flowering when the bulbs are growing sufficient moisture is available. Great advances have been made in the last 25 years in developing near perfect shape and form of the flowers and these can often be admired at the special spring daffodil shows which are organised by local horticultural societies. However for garden purposes we require varieties that are capable of producing large numbers of flowers with strong stems and constitutions. Good examples are trumpet varieties Rembrandt, solid golden yellow; Mount Hood, pure white; the large cupped varieties Delibes, rich yellow petals and red crown; and Kilworth, pure white with brilliant orange cup. Readers particularly interested in this subject should study specialist's catalogues, which give a wealth of information.

The **Tulip** family also embraces a large number of different varieties and types and when these are carefully chosen it is possible to have a continuous show for almost three months, starting with some of the Kaufmanniana varieties in March and finishing with exotic Parrot tulips with their frilled and crested petals in May. The popularity of the species tulips, which includes the Kaufmanniana and Greigii groups, continues to increase year by year. This is no doubt due to their short sturdy growth averaging 30cm/12in in height and their beautifully marked foliage which is an added attraction before as well as after flowering. Perhaps the most popular of all is Red Riding Hood with its waisted blooms of brilliant scarlet and heavily mottled foliage. Darwin Hybrids are a race resulting from a cross between Darwins and Fosterianas. They produce enormous flowers carried on stout stems about 60cm/24in long, blooming during late April in advance of the Darwins, their rich colours creating a dazzling effect. Apeldoorn, orange scarlet, and its golden yellow form Golden Apeldoorn are fine examples. Tulips may be planted from the end of September until December, requiring a well drained site and setting them approximately 10cm/4in deep. Their main enemies are slugs which like to eat the tender shoots as they appear through the ground and tulip fire which is a fungus present in the soil, usually caused by decaying tulip matter from previous year's plantings. To keep the soil clean it is essential therefore to remove the flower petals as they drop off and also the foliage when this begins to turn yellow. Slug damage can easily be prevented by the use of the many different types of slug bait available.

No bulbs perhaps are more appreciated than **hyacinths** which fill our homes with their delightful fragrance from Christmas onwards. For this season early varieties are used, such as L'Innocence, white; Pink Pearl, deep pink; Ostara, bright blue; these have been specially treated in warm and humidity-controlled stores to advance the embryo flower buds. A common error in the cultivation of hyacinths for indoors is to transfer them into the light and warmth too early. The time varies for different varieties, depending on whether they are naturally early or late flowering, but a good guide is to wait until the shoot is approximately 5cm/2in high, in other words when the bud is well out of the neck of the bulb. If transferred too early the bud will cease to lengthen and this will ultimately result in decay. Hyacinths are also most suitable for

A massed array of tulips is always impressive

55

Hyacinths should be planted in groups for maximum effect

tude of blossom during March-April. They are very much at home amongst the stones of a rock garden, growing to a height of about 13cm/5in, and once established there is no fear of losing them. Anemone fulgens deserves a mention as its flowers are of the brightest scarlet with a centre boss of black stamens creating a delightful contrast.

Few flowers are more treasured than the **eranthis** or aconite which can show their pretty buttercups as early as January. These should be planted 2.5cm/1in deep and in doing so select a pocket where they can be left undisturbed when they will increase rapidly. They are perfectly hardy and bad as the weather may be in the early part of the year, this will in no way deter them, making themselves excellent companions for the **snowdrops.**

Fritillaria meleagris, commonly named snake's head fritillary, is amongst the most delightful of the miscellaneous bulbs. Their bell shaped flowers in shades varying from white through rose to deep purple are borne on slender 30cm/12in stems during April, dancing in the breeze like little chinese lanterns. Plant 5cm/2in deep during September-October preferably in fairly damp soil. They are an excellent investment as they multiply well and seed themselves freely. They also make a very attractive flower for table decoration.

No garden can ever be considered complete without **crocuses,** be it the autumn flowering which commence to bloom in October, the winter flowering species and their varieties or the large Dutch crocus. They all produce a multitude of flowers. Autumn flowering crocus are perhaps the least known yet their flowers in shades of lilac and mauve with brilliant orange stigmatas look most attractive amongst the drab autumn leaves. They naturally require early planting and should be in the ground by the beginning of September. There are many winter flowering varieties blooming from January onwards but of these the chrysanthus crocus are the most beautiful. Fine examples are Blue Pearl, lovely pearly blue; Cream Beauty, rounded creamy yellow blossoms; E. A. Bowles, deep

window boxes and garden troughs but remember to water well during prolonged dry weather. If used for the garden they should be planted 10cm/4in deep and 10–13cm/4–5in apart.

The miscellaneous bulbs fill a very important part in the planning of a garden and many of them can be used for widely differing purposes. The rock garden is the foremost place for these subjects but many are equally at home planted in groups in the border or in larger drifts in the more natural parts of the garden. They multiply rapidly, some seeding themselves, so that in a reasonably short time a good stock can be obtained. We shall now discuss some of the most important of this group.

The genus of **anemone** or windflower consists of several different types but the species blanda in various shades of blue, pink and white outshines any in popularity, producing a multi-

The pretty snake's head fritillary

The crown imperial, a large relation of the snake's head fritillary

Crocuses naturalized in an informal garden

gold; all producing tufts of up to fifteen flowers; apart from outdoor planting they are most attractive in shallow pens of bowls thus remaining unblemished by the weather. Crocus tomasinianus and its varieties in shades of silver and deep purple deserve a special mention as these are the finest for naturalizing, rapidly multiplying and freely seeding themselves. Crocuses may be planted throughout the autumn, about 5cm/2in deep except for the large flowered varieties which should be set at a depth of 8cm/3in.

One of the many different forms of iris

The **galanthus** or snowdrops need little introduction as perhaps they are the most well known flowers of all. The dry bulbs may also be planted throughout the autumn, 5–8cm/2–3in deep, but when clumps have become congested they can be transplanted during the early spring; this should be done as soon as possible after flowering before the foliage turns yellow. This way they will very easily re-establish themselves.

Muscari or grape hyacinths look particularly beautiful if planted in large drifts; visitors to the Keukenhof exhibition in Holland will no doubt have seen them in their thousands, creating a magnificent carpet of blue. The most well known variety Heavenly Blue may be used for all purposes, including interplanting with tulips, a combination which looks most effective. Muscari azureum which produces tight heads of soft powder blue with short leaves grows only 15cm/16in high and is very lovely in bowls for indoors. If planted during September they will flower in January and provided they are kept on a cool window-sill will last for several weeks. Its white form, azureum album, is also most enchanting.

The same conditions as for muscari apply to **scillas,** notable varieties amongst them being bifolia, sky blue, and the taller siberica with lovely cobalt blue star shaped flowers loosely set on slender 13cm/5in stems.

Until recently **endymion** was classified as scilla, including such species as *Endymion non scriptus* commonly known as bluebell with its pink and white form. *Endymion hispanica,* also known as scilla campanulata or Spanish bluebell, is much more robust than the former, colours include various shades of blue, pink and white. Both are ideal for planting at a depth of 8cm/13in in the natural part of the garden, where they will seed themselves freely and produce a multitude of flowers during May.

For readers who are in possession of a greenhouse **freesias** are amongst the most lovely flowers one can grow, their gorgeous colours and delicious scent having no equal. It must be emphasized however that they are not suitable for growing in the house. The best time to plant is during September in 13cm/5in pots, which should be plunged in the garden up to the rim. By mid-October they may be transferred to the greenhouse giving a temperature of 10°C/50° Fahrenheit which may gradually be increased to 15°C/60°F. The secret of success is not too much heat and plenty of ventilation when they will produce large sprays of lasting flowers on strong stems.

Summer Bulbs

We will now briefly discuss some of the more popular summer flowering bulbs which are well worth growing. **Anemone** single Caen and its double form St. Brigid come first to mind, these are ideal for flower decoration and very easily grown. They prefer a rich well drained soil and may be planted from March onwards, 8cm/3in deep. It takes approximately 100 days from planting until flowering and so by staggering planting time a succession of blooms may be obtained. The magnificent multicoloured **ranunculus** with their large double flowers in almost every conceivable shade require similar conditions. People often wonder how to plant these curious corms and the answer to this is claws downwards.

In the last few years **lilies** have become very popular and this is no doubt due to the introduction of many new varieties raised in the United States. These are much less particular in

A spring bulb scene

their cultural requirements than the old species, in fact with only a reasonable amount of care excellent results can be obtained. Lilies may be planted from November to March but a well drained site is essential; in very limey soils plenty of leaf-mould and peat should be added. Set the bulbs at a depth of 13–15cm/5–6in; this is essential for the stem roots to develop, as many varieties not only produce roots at the base of the bulbs but also from the stem. The majority of

Lilies come in many different colours and forms

Dahlias will not survive any frost, but are well worth growing

lilies flower during June–July, varying in height from 1–2m/3–6ft, but the season is extended well into the end of August by the speciosum hybrids. The range and type are so extensive that it is best to consult a specialist catalogue to select your requirements.

Among really choice plants **nerines** well deserve a place. Bowdenii is the most commonly grown with its strap like foliage and large umbels of soft pink flowers in September. Apart from the mildest parts of the country they are not reliably winter hardy and should therefore be covered with a thick layer of bracken during the winter months but remove this in the spring. The ideal place is in front of a wall facing south, planting the bulbs with their tip just below ground level.

The tuberous **begonias** should be grown much more extensively as they produce a multitude of fine blooms in jewel-like colours from July until the first night frosts. They are not hardy and the best plan therefore is to start the tubers off in boxes in the greenhouse or garden shed in March and plant out at the end of May or June according to local conditions. Lift the tubers after the first frost and store during the winter in a frost-free place. The large flowered begonias are ideal for bedding while the smaller multiflora type are most suitable for the rock garden or narrow borders; the pendulous begonias look most effective in hanging baskets or window boxes. To obtain best results plant in rich soil and water abundantly, pre-ferably in the early morning or during the evening.

Dahlias are valuable garden plants giving a wealth of blooms throughout the summer and early autumn and as cut flowers they are unsurpassed at that time of the year. The tubers may be planted in a sunny part of the garden in May or earlier according to local conditions. They will produce several shoots but only three or four of the strongest should be retained. An alternative method of culture is to plant the tubers on the bench in the greenhouse in February–March taking cuttings as they develop, while making sure to include a small part of the tuber as this will facilitate rooting. After the initial period in the greenhouse they may be potted and transferred to a cold frame, keeping them frost free until it is safe to plant out in the garden. The majority of dahlias will grow to a height of 1–2m/3–6ft and it is therefore advisable to put in a stake for each at the time of planting out. Dahlias are by nature hungry and some organic manure should therefore be incorporated in the soil. As soon as possible after the first frost in the autumn lift the tubers, remove the old growth and store covered by slightly damp peat or sand in a frost free place. The most popular types are the decoratives which produce rounded rather formal flowers and the cactus type, with their characteristic spiky petals; pompons are also an important group but because of their small flowers are more suited for cutting than garden display.

9 Climbing Plants

The planting of walls, pergolas, arches and trellis work with suitable plants is an important part of gardening, and deserves special consideration.

Planting

If you are planting at the base of a wall, the soil may well be of poor quality and contain subsoil or broken bricks, and if this is so, good soil in the form of loam should be substituted. It is also important to remember that the soil at the foot of a wall will tend to be much drier than other parts of the garden, and you should not forget to water. The old fashioned method of attaching climbing plants to walls with nails looks ugly, and may well damage the bricks; the best thing is to fix a wooden trellis to the wall, but tightly stretched wires are just as good.

After care

Wall plants often need extra care during their first season. A good mulch of garden compost or well rotted manure should be given to conserve moisture, and some protection against frost may be needed.

Pruning and Training

Unless pruning and training are correctly carried out the whole effect of your wall, trellis or pergola may be spoilt. The object of training is to cover a bare surface, but not completely, and of course it is important to keep windows free.

Shrub-like plants, such as wisteria, should be trained out to give cover where required, and have all shoots cut back annually to within two or three buds. Wisteria is best pruned just after leaf fall, but berrying shrubs should have unwanted shoots cut out in the early autumn in order to expose the fruits.

For clematis, correct pruning and training is very important. The early flowering ones should be carefully spaced out to give a basic framework; this will probably take at least two years. After the first year they should be cut back to within 60cm/24in of the ground; this should be done in August.

The later flowering varieties are pruned in February just as growth commences by cutting back young shoots to two or three buds.

In the training of wall plants care must be taken to ensure that no woody stems are allowed to grow between the wall and any down pipes, as this will eventually cause trouble.

Rambler roses are not suited to wall training, but are very valuable for arches, pergolas or trellises. Each year when flowering is finished they should be taken down from their supports, and the old flowered growths should be cut out completely. The young wood should then be evenly tied in over the space available. Both ramblers and climbers when newly planted should be cut back fairly hard in March.

List of Climbing Plants

Actinidia kolomikta A deciduous climber growing to 6m/20ft, with greenish white flowers about 1cm/½in across, and oblong leaves about

Climbing plants should be kept clear
of house windows

Climbing roses can be used to
disguise an unsightly building

Above: the ever-popular clematis
Left: a climbing vine

15cm/6in long. Flowers in early summer, followed by yellow berries. Best on a south or west facing wall.

Campsis (Trumpet creeper) *C. grandiflora* is a deciduous climber growing to 9m/30ft, with funnel shaped orange flowers in August and September. *C. × tagliabuana* is a deciduous climber, very vigorous, reaching 10·5m/25ft, with 10cm/4in long scarlet flowers in August and September. Does best in hot climates.

Celastrus orbiculatus is a very vigorous deciduous climber growing to 12m/40ft. Small yellow flower June to August, slightly toothed leaves about 13cm/5in long. Very spectacular fruits in the autumn and winter.

Clematis These are generally considered to do best when there roots are in shade and their heads in sun. *C. armandii* is an evergreen climber to 6m/20ft, large clusters of white star shaped flowers in spring. *C. heracleifolia* has blue flowers in summer. *C. montana* is a very vigorous deciduous climber reaching 9m/30ft, with white star shaped flowers in spring. Some of the large flowered hybrid clematis are: pink, Comtesse de Bouchaud, Nelly Moser; white, Henryi; blue, Jackmanii, Lasurstern; red, Ville de Lyon.

Clianthus puniceus (Parrot's Bill) An evergreen climbing shrub reaching 3·5m/12ft. Large red flowers in clusters in summer, not very hardy.

Cobaea scandens Not hardy, and therefore generally grown outdoors as an annual. Violet bell-shaped flowers 8cm/3in long from June to September.

Jasminum polyanthum A very vigorous climber, with white or pink flowers from April to June. Usually grown as a cool greenhouse plant, but will succeed against south facing walls in warmer parts of the UK.

Lonicera (Honeysuckle) *L.* × *americana* has creamy white flowers with a pink tinge, June to August. *L.* × *brownii* has orange-scarlet flowers in summer. *L. periclymenum* (woodbine) has large clusters of creamy white flowers in summer.

Passiflora caerulea (Passion Flower) is a vigorous evergreen climber, tender in cold districts. It has star shaped flowers up to 7cm/2½in wide, greenish white with blue stamens in the centre.

Roses See a list of suggested climbing varieties on page 73.

Vitis (Vine) *V. coignetiae* is a very vigorous climber which can be grown over old trees or hedges, and can reach 18m/60ft. It is grown for its brilliant crimson and scarlet foliage in autumn, with leaves up to 25cm/10in long by 20cm/8in wide.

Wisteria *W. floribunda* has blue, purple or lilac flowers in early summer. *W. sinensis* is a deciduous woody climber with mauve flowers in late spring.

10 Roses

Roses have been loved in many different lands, and for longer than anyone can trace. Their popular title, Queen of Flowers, is already two thousand years old and more. It was earned by the fragrance and endearing shape of the blooms.

Fortunately roses are easy plants to grow, and a lot of people manage without reading any cultural instructions at all. But it is possible to grow them better in the light of knowledge, especially if we know why we do certain things.

Planting Roses

For instance, in choosing where to plant roses, why are we told to choose a sunny place, preferably with some shelter from the wind? The reason is that sunlight starts the green granules within the plant into movement, and thus switches on the whole complex chemical activity of growth. Take away the sunlight, and the switch goes off. In strong wind, the leaves are being whipped about in and out of the sunlight, and the growth process is frequently interrupted, consequently slow, and thus the plants are short. Therefore it is clear that the position for optimum results is a sunny one, with kindly windbreaks; and to the extent these conditions are not provided, so the results fall short of what they could be, although they may still be reasonably pleasing.

The quest for the ideal soil is similarly clear. It has maximum fertility and depth, and a fine constituency. Fertility and depth speak for themselves, being no more than quality and quantity, both capable of reinforcement if necessary. Constituency is not so well understood, until we look at the roots. They chiefly absorb minerals in solution through pores on their skin, by sucking from moist soil. But they cannot such out of air. That is why the soil needs to fit firmly against the roots, instead of lying in great clods separated by air pockets. There is enough air for the roots among grains of sand.

Roses adapt themselves to many soils, and we may at once say there are only two kinds of soil for which one would do best not even to think of roses. One is a waterlogged soil, and the other an excessively poor, acid one. In water, the pores of the roots are covered and choked by slime, and the roots rot. From poor, very acid soils, the rose fails to mine the elements it needs as fuel for its growth activities. Having dismissed these two soils, we are left with nearly the whole range of known soils to plant roses in; and as we know that the root pores need to be in close contact with the soil, we also know how to prepare the soil for planting. It must be broken up finely, and that means digging.

Digging is a delicate job, in which the soil must be turned over, and yet remain with the topsoil above, and the subsoil below. It has to be tailored to the material, for a heavy soil can only be worked when the weather is exactly right, whereas a light one is more often accessible. Heavy soils need careful timing, and very likely more than one cultivation if they have not been broken recently. After digging, the help of nature is necessary, to crumble the soil further by frosts and thaws, wettings and dryings, until gravity fills the air pockets left by the spade. If in the course of preparation good manure or

Hybrid tea roses are a comparatively recent introduction

compost is mixed with the soil, the fertility will be increased in proportion.

At planting time, remember three maxims: plant firmly; plant wet roots; plant at the correct depth.

Plant firmly, because we know the soil must be close to the roots. Let the roots run more or less horizontally at the bottom of the planting hole. Cover them with fine soil, and tread firmly. A hole 15–18cm/6 or 7in deep is enough for an average young rose plant. Do not dig deeper than necessary, or you will leave air pockets under the roots. Give the plant a tug after it is planted, to ensure it holds firm.

Plant wet roots, because then the soil will stick to them right away. Dry roots stay dry long after being planted, almost as if they had repelled the soil, and are wearing a jacket of air

instead. There's no need to soak the roots for hours (unless your plants are half dead); a twirl in a bucket of water will do.

Plant at the correct depth: for all but standard roses, that depth is where the root growth and shoot growth meet. That point should be at soil level, or 3cm/1in below; not above. Thus the plant is properly anchored, and the light can still incite growth from the most vital source of new growth, the plant's base. For standard roses, bury only as much of the stem as is necessary to make the plant stand straight. Deep planting does standards no good at all. And it is well to hammer in a stake before planting standards.

When planting a number of roses, one soon gets the knack of using the soil from hole number two to fill up the plant in hole number one. The average planting distance to make a massed rose bed is 2 feet apart. It is not safe to scatter fertilizers on the roots, which are better surrounded by fine soil, or a planting mixture.

Pruning

Anyone might think pruning a profound science, judging by all that is written about it. It is very simple, and provided we know why we do it, we can soon see that we are only copying nature. Pruning is merely discarding the parts of the plant which are inefficient; and nature had her own drastic ways of doing it. She froze the immature shoots and burnt the old, dry or dead ones. Surely we can do nothing worse, with our sharp wits and secateurs?

Roses are woody plants, with a natural way of springing from the base. They do not expect to keep their shoots for ever, and their urge for renewal is founded upon the expectation of accidents, and on the necessity to survive them. Thus their sap is fickle, following new channels, and forsaking the old. But the wood is stored with carbohydrates, won from the air and the soil, manufactured into plant food, and stored away by the remarkable energy of plant growth. It is a sin and a shame to cut such wood off, and burn it prematurely. You might just as well re-order a house by demolishing the kitchen and larder.

Therefore, when you prune, begin by thinking about the plant's food stores, and ask yourself where they are? They are in the firm, thick

Roses do best in a slightly heavy soil

wood, whether young (and green) or older (and dark). Obviously we shall keep all the young thick wood we can; and the test of the older wood is to see if it is still bearing young wood. If it has no good shots arising from it, then the old wood should be cut out, either in part, or completely to the base, according to whether you think it still has a chance or not.

This will leave the sound old wood, together with all the younger wood carried upon it. The next stage of pruning is to shorten the young wood, and the reason for doing so is to make it bear flowers from the stouter part of it, which of course is towards its base. A reasonable rule of thumb is to cut the young shoots at a point where you think they are as thick as the sort of stem you would like to put in a vase.

This will result in your pruning less severely than is usually recommended; it will also mean you are pruning for the kind of flowers you like; and with experience you will find yourself adjusting your pruning to suit varieties of different stem thicknesses. However there is one overriding factor which governs pruning in Britain, and it is frost. All too often, after cutting at the desired point, the pruner finds that frost has pinched the pith brown and dry. In that case, one must cut lower until white, fresh pith is reached. All too often, this means that the plant ends up very short indeed.

Some general details about pruning: the best time is early spring, before there is much growth. The cuts should be made closely above an eye, on the slant, the eye being on the higher side of the slant. If you cannot see an eye, cut just the same, and go round a few weeks later to remove any stubs you have left. You will, incidentally, then observe the line the wood takes as it dies back to the eye, and this teaches how to copy nature when you make that slanting cut another time. Burn prunings promptly, before pests migrate back to the roses, or other creatures make nests in the pile. You may choose to vary your methods to govern the shape

Above: the hybrid tea rose 'Super Star'
Below: cut off the flower heads as they fade

'Peace'–this rose has been so
successful that it is known
throughout the world under
various names

or size of your plant; for instance, if it is too tall, cut it down. Climbers and ramblers may be quickly pruned by shearing the side shoots back, although the day is bound to come when some of the older parts have to be painfully extricated.

It is as well to prune newly planted roses quite hard, leaving bushes three to six inches high, shrubs and climbers up to about two feet, and standards about six inches beyond the unions on top of the stem. The reason for this alteration from general practice is that the roots need a few months before they can adequately sustain all the growth the stems are willing to initiate. Therefore we reduce the number of eyes on the stems to agree with what the roots can support.

After pruning, the soil should be put in order, by removing weeds, and either hoeing or chipping it, to make a fine tilth on top. One of the worst things you can do to roses is to dig around

them, and the next worst is to trample the soil so much that it needs digging. When tidying a rose bed, if it is too consolidated to hoe, use a small sharp spade, and just chip the soil surface, holding the spade almost vertical, and making chips close together and about 3cm/1in deep. After a few dry days, the bed should hoe down nicely; and you could take the chance of putting on some rose fertilizer, and hoeing it in at the same time. Be careful, when working among the roses, not to knock them with tools, because the injuries so caused may seriously impede the flow of sap, which travels just inside the bark; they may also admit canker spores from the soil, and cause trouble later on.

Do not leave labels tied round the base of the plants. They are sure to be forgotten, and when found a few years later, their string (or, worse still, wire) may be strangling the plant.

Feeding

As the roses grow, even their young leaves are a delight, and one's instinct is to help them along with food. There are several good rose fertilizers on the market, and they may be applied at intervals of about a month, from after spring pruning, up to late June, when you should stop. Try to avoid doing it in dry, windy weather, or lese the fertilizer will blow away. It is best applied when the soil is damp, or just before it is going to rain. Early applications may be applied on a frosty morning–the fertilizer goes down with the thaw.

Foliar feed is useful, because it is very quickly available to the plants, being sprayed on the leaves, which take it in at once. Therefore it can be a tonic to any plants which seem in need, also to those which do not appear to benefit from fertilizer, as often occurs on highly alkaline soils. It may be applied when the plants have sufficient leaves to catch it, and up to late summer to help the autumn flowers.

Mulches add humus to the soil, which otherwise may get very little in all the years the roses occupy it. They may be of rotted manure, compost, or peat. Manure or compost are best put on after pruning, and chipped in with a spade, as already described. Peat, having no immediate food value, may be applied when the roses are nicely started into growth, for the soil will then be warmed up, and there is no virtue in insulating cold soil with a layer of peat.

There are no set rules about fertilizing by one or the other of these three methods. Rather it is a matter of suiting one's inclination and pocket, and learning by trial which method, or combination of methods, gives the results one likes.

Pests and Diseases

Of the pests and diseases to watch for, greenfly is the most common, mildew and blackspot the most annoying, and rust the most dangerous. The first three are easy to see, but rust often escapes notice. Watch out for it on the lower leaves, and if you see yellow dots, like pin pricks, look under the leaf. Rust grows there, in groups of orange pustules, which turn black when mature. Elsewhere in this book is a section on pests and diseases, to which you may refer for remedies. But so far as roses go, remember they have a strong instinct to survive, and if you think something has ruined your roses, you can usually cut it off, burn it, and find the plants will grow again. Then perhaps next year, you will put on the cure in time. A plant which consistently gives trouble should be discarded, because you can soon spend more money on spraying than on buying another rose bush.

Most roses are growing on the roots of a wild rose, which occasionally sends up suckers. Do not believe the old story that they can be identified by the number of their leaflets; seven is the usual tale, and it is highly unreliable. The surest way is the point of origin. If it is from the rootstock, it is sucker; if from the rose, it is rose. But don't forget the stem of a standard counts as rootstock for this purpose. Suckers should be pulled or rubbed out as soon as seen, otherwise they become woody, and are more difficult to get rid of.

An old-fashioned shrub rose, *Rosa moyesii*

Above: a standard rose bush
Left: climbing roses are excellent for growing up pergolas

Below: roses covering a bare wall

To obtain subsequent crops of flower more rapidly, remove the old flowers when they cease to please. This encourages the plant to grow again, instead of peacefully setting seed.

Varieties

This review of how to grow roses would be incomplete without giving some hint of the wonderful beauty which the genus offers. The starting point for most people is **hybrid tea** roses, either as bushes or standards; the large, high centred blooms of hybrid teas are, in popular estimation, true and traditional roses. In fact, they are only about a century old. Some of the most resplendent to grow at the time of writing are in red: 'Alec's Red' and 'Red Devil'; in scarlet: 'Alexander' and 'Fragrant Cloud'; in pink: 'Silver Jubilee' and 'Wendy Cussons'; in orange salmon: 'Just Joey' and 'Typhoon'; in yellow: 'Grandpa Dickson' and 'Sunblest'; in near white: 'Elizabeth Harkness' and 'Pascali'; and in lilac 'Blue Moon'.

Beautiful as hybrid teas are, there is a temptation to have a riotous sea of colour, and **floribundas** are the roses for that purpose. Their flowers vary in doubleness, but have the common factor of flowering in large heads very abundantly. The superb ones today are in red: 'Evelyn Fison' and 'Rob Roy'; in scarlet: 'Orange Sensation' and 'Trumpeter'; in pink: 'Pink Parfait' and 'Queen Elizabeth' (which is tall); in orange salmon: 'Redgold' and 'Southampton'; in yellow: 'Korresia' and 'Sunsilk'; in near white: 'Iced Ginger' and 'Iceberg'; and in lilac: 'Escapade' and 'News'.

Small gardens ask for small neat plants, which in roses may be had from short growing floribundas and from **miniatures,** the latter having tiny leaves in proportion. Some of the best are in red: 'Marlena' (Flor); in scarlet: 'Starina' (Min); in pink: 'New Penny' (Min) and 'Royal Salute' (Flor); in yellow and salmon: 'Baby Masquerade' (Min); in yellow: 'Rosina' (Min); and in near white: 'Easter Morning' (Min).

Roses are glorious **shrubs,** and there is a fantastic range of beautiful plants among them, outside the commonly seen garden varieties. The beginner could well plant 'Canary Bird', *R. moyesii* 'Geranium' and *R. rugosa scabrosa,* and see if he is not tempted to adventure further.

The best **climbing roses** are perhaps: in red: 'Parkdirektor Riggers'; in scarlet: 'Altissimo'; in pink: 'Handel' (pink and white) and 'Pink Perpetue'; in orange salmon: 'Compression'; in yellow: 'Golden Showers'; and in cream: 'Mermaid'.

To conclude: when the beauty of roses has enriched anyone's life, he is in company with his ancestors behond any genealogist's tracing; and a very sensible step is to join also his contemporaries, by becoming a member of the Royal National Rose Society at St. Albans.

11 Trees, Shrubs and Hedges

Trees

Trees play a very important role in providing an environment that is pleasant to enjoy and live in. Imagine our situation particularly in urban areas, with innumerable high rise buildings, densely populated zones, without trees. They do much to absorb noise, grit, dust and other atmospheric pollutants, thus providing us with a slightly cleaner, quieter place to live. How stark and drab urban areas would be without the occasional 'green belt' of colour provided by trees.

Selection

The choice of tree is naturally a personal matter. Selection is based either on advice from nurseries, garden suppliers, reading literature, or more often than not personal observation. When choosing trees particularly for the smaller garden, selection is vitally important. A small 1·8m/6ft standard tree may look harmless enough for the first few years, but what one must envisage is 20 years hence, when the tree may have developed into an invasive, overshadowing nuisance. Trees which are notorious in this respect and often wrongly planted include many of the types which attain large proportions later in life. In confined areas the Elms *Ulmus,* Willows *Salix,* and Poplars *Populus* must be avoided at all costs. Not only will they ultimately make large trees, but all have shown tendency to drop or shed large limbs without warning. Furthermore below ground on clay soils roots may cause soil shrinkage, resulting in damage to foundations and structures. Remember the majority of trees have equal or greater root spread than branch spread, so avoid planting too close to buildings, and check on the plant's ultimate spread at maturity.

We are fortunate in having an amicable climate suiting a wide range of very diverse ornamental trees. All possess certain decorative features whether in flower, fruits, leaf colour, shape, or bark to provide attraction at certain times of the year. Selection therefore combines not only the practical aspects of soil type, size of garden, climate and siting, but choosing and combining features to create interest throughout the year.

Once a choice has been made considering all the factors, the tree should be allowed to develop naturally without danger of encroaching on nearby buildings, fences, or roadways, thus causing possible nuisance to others. If space is very limiting always find out the ultimate height and spread at maturity before purchasing. Having found this information selection then becomes a simple task of finding a suitable tree to meet your particular requirement within a given area. Even the smallest patio or garden can accommodate the right type of tree. The extremely narrow upright, pale pink, spring flowering cherry, *Prunus 'Amanogawa'* is rarely wider than 1m/3ft through; similar in habit is the pencil cedar *Juniperus virginiana* 'Skyrocket' with its columnar clusters of upright blue grey foliage ascending towards the sky. In terms of value in sheer beauty and diversity, few other commodities can offer so much, for such low initial outlay as the tree. It is often possible to combine several different features from one

Lilac

carefully chosen plant. Often subjects selected for a single quality, possibly spring flower, do little to justify their position for the rest of the year. If at all possible, particularly where space restricts you to one tree, choose wisely to produce interest and diversity through the year for everyone to admire and enjoy. Having taken delivery of the tree the next consideration must be planting.

Planting

The main planting season is between October and March when the majority of subjects are dormant or resting. Exact timing is entirely dependent on weather and soil conditions. Always ensure that during unfavourable periods when high winds, freezing temperatures, or waterlogged soils may delay planting, the tree is 'heeled in', that is, placed in a sheltered area in a shallow trench with its roots protected until conditions improve. If the roots have been allowed to dry out always soak them in water before planting.

To facilitate optimum conditions for establishment the soil must be well cultivated prior to planting and free from all weeds particularly perennials including nettles, docks and brambles. A normal standard tree must have a hole of at least 1m/3ft across with a depth of 0·5m/20in. If planting in turf mark out a circle with a peg and line from the central point, lift and remove the turf completely. When removing the soil from the pit always keep the top and subsoil in separate piles on polythene or hessian sacking. The subsoil is usually much lighter in colour. If the sides of the hole look compact and 'glazed', remove this by lightly piercing with a fork. Equally important is to fork over the base of the pit, thus improving drainage and encouraging good root development.

With the pit excavated decide if the tree requires support or staking. This operation must be carried out before planting to avoid possible root damage to the newly planted tree. Choose a sturdy treated chestnut, larch or pine stake, and ensure it stands firmly in a vertical position.

Planting generally requires two persons, one to position and hold the tree, while a second back-fills with good topsoil. Check the tree for any broken or damaged roots, and assess the correct planting depth. This is critical and controlled by locating the soil mark or 'line' situated just above the root collar. Always plant at the same depth at which the tree was previously grown. Having located the 'line' the person holding the tree must keep this level with the top of the hole until planting is finished. Spread the roots out equally around the base of the hole, while one person starts backfilling with topsoil. The person holding the tree must carefully shake it to encourage soil to settle around the root system. Firming should take place with the ball of the foot as each 40cm/16in layer of soil is returned to the hole. With all the soil replaced and finally firmed lay a 25mm mulch of peat or leaf-mould around the base of the plant. This provides extra plant foods, cools the soil, keeps down weed populations and retains moisture.

Staking

After planting trees must be secured to the stakes by tying with any of the proprietary tree ties. Generally two will suffice, one positioned 1cm/$\frac{1}{2}$in from the top of the stake with a second halfway down to straighten a misshapen stem. Ties are secured by nailing to stakes but rubbing will occur unless 'buffers' or spacers are placed between the stake and tree in order to prevent friction.

Aftercare

Immediately after planting trees must be thoroughly watered. During the initial establishment period it is essential to keep the base of the tree weed free. Check all tree ties after 9–12 months for any signs of construction or stem damage. Irrigate as required particularly during hot dry summers. Remove the stake after 2–3 years depending on how well trees have established and developed. If any of these maintenance operations are neglected trees may ultimately die.

The Trees

Perhaps the most widely planted group are the flowering cherries. Most are selected for spring flower, but others exhibit special qualities like *Prunus sargentii,* one of the best of all cherries for a blaze of autumn colour. Another favourite small tree which differs from the majority is *Prunus subhistella 'Autumnalis'* which produces periodic winter flowers from November to March during milder weather. A more attractive striking tree is the spring flowering common almond, *Prunus dulcis,* a complete haze of rich pink in early April, followed by interesting fruit later in season. It rarely exceeds 9m/30ft in height and with a spread of 6m/20ft is most suited to small gardens.

The flowering crabs *Malus* also feature in the spring display with many spectacular varieties in the group. Of particular note are *Malus* 'Golden Hornet' covered in a mass of pure white single flowers in May yet saving its major feature, a superb show of bright yellow fruits, until early winter. The most popular of the crabs is *Malus* 'John Downie' a small tree to 6m/20ft with a spread of 4m/14ft and having masses of eyecatching, edible, orange red fruits which follow the summer display of white flower.

In the same family, the Rosaceae, are the ornamental pears, *Pyrus.* Undoubtedly a very popular feature plant from this group is the willow leaved Pear *Pyrus salicifolia 'Pendula'.* This attractive small fairly slow growing tree has silver-grey pendulous branches which in April support the display of white flowers. Small brown fruits are sometimes seen in winter.

For a different effect during winter certain trees are selected for decorative bark. The paper bark maple *Acer griseum* is a slow growing tree to 9m/30ft with flaky brown bark which peels to reveal a beautiful cinnamon coloured stem. Equally stunning is the Tibetan cherry *Prunus serrula* with its shiny, almost polished mahogany brown trunk and stem. Both are best planted where winter sunshine can illuminate the spectacular bark.

Autumn provides a time when no garden should be without colour. Here the maples in all

Above: many dwarf conifers are available for small gardens
Right: a conifer garden

their glory do most to provide this. Again *Acer griseum* with its small trifoliate leaves has a special colouring of deep red during October. In the group the Japanese maples possess some glorious shades in particular the *Acer palmatum* section with every conceivable colouration from pale yellow through to deep purple. *Acer palmatum 'Senkaki'* is perhaps the most accommodating in the smaller garden as it rarely reaches more than 3m/10ft and spreads no more than half its height. The palmate green leaves turn to yellows and golds before falling and revealing decorative coral red stems and shoots.

Another tree noted for its autumn richness is *Rhys typhina* the sumach, or stag's horn. This species makes a small broad spreading tree of some 6m/20ft across, producing large pinnate leaves to 600mm/2ft in length. These turn magnificent shades of red and gold in late October and on female trees clustered heads of terminal fruits are seen. After the leaves are shed berries and fruit provide winter decoration in the garden and food for wild life. The *Sorbus* are a group noted for colourful displays of large and small berries with out native mountain ash *Sorbus aucuparia* leading the way with great hanging clusters of orange fruits. The Chinese mountain ash *Sorbus hupehensis* provides a

backcloth of rich red autumn colour to enhance the superb display of rosy white fruits which maintain interest well into winter; perhaps one of the better less-known trees which rarely exceeds 9m/30ft with a spread of 4–5m/13–16ft. Hopefully we may see more of these choice, yet easy to grow trees replacing some of the commoner types in the next decade.

Shrubs

With the increasing interest in low maintenance gardening, shrubs provide an ideal medium to achieve this and create beautiful effects. Their diversity in providing flowers for every season, fruits and berries in winter glorious shades of leaf colour during autumn means no garden should ever be without colour and interest. By carefully planning a garden it is possible to combine the aesthetic beauty of plants and utilize their natural covering habit to reduce maintenance cost. Obviously the bigger the garden the more important it is to keep these costs to a minimum.

Planning the Border
Where new shrub borders are intended it is advisable to prepare a simple plan detailing

Buddleia, the butterfly bush

exactly what is to be planted where it will look effective, and with what it will combine well. Obvious considerations must be the ultimate height and spread of plants being used. There are many permutations one can try with plants, possibly use of contrasting foliage, shapes, size or simple colour combinations using flowers or foliage.

Above all avoid 'bitty' planting, using single plants dotted at random over the garden. Nothing looks more unattractive and completely disjointed. Try where possible to plant in groups however small–threes or fives can look very effective and produce a bolder massed effect. A point worth remembering is to select subjects which will provide interest in the border throughout the year. With such a variety of plants on the market this should not be difficult. Prior to planting set plants out in their positions and assess whether anything looks drastically out of place.

Planting

The basic principles are similar to those out-

lined for trees, differing mainly in size of root system. This does not mean shrubs can be squeezed into tiny holes. They must be wide and deep enough adequately to accommodate the root system, thus allowing space for new root development. If the plants, particularly bare rooted types have been standing around for some time, ensure they are well soaked before planting. It is advisable to cut away any hessian or root wrap as this may well restrict root growth if left.

Container grown plants cannot be left in pots unless they are of the degradable type. If in any doubt remove them just prior to planting. Always aim to plant shrubs at the precise depth at which they have previously been grown, checking the depth of the hole before backfilling with soil. If possible plant when soils are moist and the sky overcast–not terribly difficult conditions to find in a typical British winter!

Try to keep to your planned spacing as this should ensure each shrub has room to develop, accepting that in 4–5 years it may require judicious pruning to keep them in bounds. By astute selection and spacing it should not be many years before shrubs begin to repay costs by effectively covering the ground thus reducing need for regular weeding and maintenance. When the planting operation is finished water everything thoroughly, lightly fork out foot marks leaving the border neat and tidy.

Aftercare

A top dressing or mulch of well rotted compost or peat is always beneficial as it provides plants with extra food, prevents loss of moisture at the root, cools the soil and restricts weed growth. In general little in the way of maintenance except to keep them weed free until they are able to spread naturally and suppress weeds themselves.

Pruning

Not all shrubs benefit from regular pruning. There are several vital points one needs to know before attempting to prune. Firstly a knowledge of when the plant flowers, what type or age of wood it flowers on, and finally how much if any wood can be safely removed without spoiling the plant. The time of flowering and type of wood obviously governs when and how much to cut without fear of losing flowers. Shrubs like camellia, hamamelis and daphne resent having much, if any wood removed, and are therefore best left unpruned. The periodic removal of all dead, diseased, or dying wood does much to improve the general health of shrub by allowing freer air movement within the plant.

Of the shrubs that require annual pruning we can roughly divide these into two groups. Those flowering on new wood produced in the same season like *Buddleia, Caryopteris,* and certain *Spiraeas,* are best cut back to a framework in March with the complete removal of all finished flowering shoots. The new shoots which emerge provide flowers later on in the season. Failure to prune these types annually results in fewer, smaller flowers. Another group of shrubs responding to cutting hard to within 5cm/2in of ground level each year are those grown specifically for winter stem colour. Most of the shrubby willows *Salix spp* and many *Cornus* benefit from 'stooling' each spring. Never attempt to prune until after winter when maximum stem effect is seen.

The second major group are shrubs which flower on wood produced in previous seasons on two or three year old plants. Within this group are spring and summer flowering types, but both require pruning as soon after flowering as possible. Here the majority of younger flowering shoots are cut back by half, and any old woody basal growth must be removed to encourage new breaks from below. Any growth produced in the later half of the season forms the basis for flower in the following year. Of the spring flowering types *Forsythia, Abeliophyllum,* and *Ribes* are pruned as flowers fade while *Philadelphus* Mock orange, *Weigela,* and *Deutzia* represent the summer flowering plants.

Evergreens rarely require much in the way of extensive pruning. Perhaps the odd shaping from time to time, and occasionally when a specimen outgrows its situation drastic steps may have to be taken. Here overgrown evergreens can be cut back to within 3cm/1in of ground level just before growth commences around April or May. Certain evergreen *Prunus* and *Rhododendrons* respond to this treatment, however it must only be practised as a last resort to keep plants to given areas. When pruning or cutting any of the larger leaved types it is wise to use secateurs, not shears which may damage leaf tissue.

Tools

A vitally important aspect of pruning is the use of sharp tools, generally secateurs or knives. Blunt or damaged implements may result in bruising or damage to stems of shrubs. This often leads to slower healing of cuts thus allowing more time for disease to colonise any exposed untreated areas. Good clean cuts always heal far quicker than dirty, damaged, cuts. Always ensure that pruning tools are the correct type for the job. Never force small secateurs trying to cut a thick shoot. If it is too large choose something more suitable like a small hand pruning saw. When making a cut on a shoot try to leave at least 1cm/½in above the bud, with a slight slope angled away from the bud to permit water runoff.

Finally any cuts made into wood of more than 1cm/½in diameter must be treated with a fungicidal tree paint sealant to protect the shrub from infection.

Shrubs for Year-Round Display

Winter Flower

Winter Sweet (*Chimonanthus praecox*)
Deciduous shrub to 3m/10ft. *Fls* waxy yellow, stained purple, highly scented. Prefers a sunny position to ripen wood, will tolerate most soils including chalk.

Witch Hazel (*Hamamelis*)
A beautiful group of slow growing deciduous shrubs. Grows well in any fertile soil in a sunny or partially shaded position. *Fls* mainly yellow, some orange through to red from November to March.

Viburnum farreri
A delightfully scented very hardy deciduous shrub to 2.4m/8ft. Free flowering in any open well drained position. Pink in bud opening white November–February.

Spring Flower

Camellia
A large group of very attractive evergreens with drak green shiny *lvs*. Best grown in a semi-shaded situation. Many fine cultivars of *Camellia japonica* can be found. *C.j.* 'Adolphe Audusson' has large semi-double deep red *fls*. Perhaps most popular of all *C. williamsii* 'Donation' a delicate free flowering double pink type.

Daphne
A group of neat compact sweetly scented spring

Above left: witch hazel
Above: potentilla
Left: a fine camellia

flowering shrubs. *D. burkwoodii* is one of the best and longest lived with pale mauve-pink *fls* in May. *D. mezereum*–deciduous *fls* February–March, scented, reddish-purple before *lvs* appear.

Star Magnolia *(Magnolia stellata)*
One of the many beautiful Magnolias forming a dense low branchwork. Ideal for small gardens as it rarely exceeds 3m/10ft. *Fls* white with strap-shaped petals very profuse March–April. Prone to spring frost damage. Prefers a sunny situation on most reasonable soils.

Summer Flower

Mexican Orange Blossom *(Choisya ternata)*
A neat round shaped evergreen shrub to 1.5m/5ft. *Fls* white highly scented May–June. Prefers a sunny fairly sheltered position on a good loam soil.

Potentilla fruticosa
A good ground covering type requiring an open sunny situation, forming dense compact bushes covered in golden yellow *fls* from mid-summer to autumn. Many cultivars seen with *fls* from yellow, white, orange and the very recent *P.* 'Red Ace' with dark red *fls*. Tolerant of any good well drained soil.

Mock Orange *(Philadelphus coronarius)*
A common name referring to the remarkable likeness of the flower scent to the *Citrus*. All very hardy, easily grown, tolerating acid or alkaline in sunny position. *Fls* June–July scented, yellowish white.

Autumn Colour

Smoke Bush *(Cotinus coggygria*
A slow growing very decorative deciduous shrub to 3m/10ft. Common name from hazy look of persistent dead flower heads. *Lvs* turn remarkable shades of deep crimson and red in autumn. Prefers a well drained soil in a sunny position.

Fothergilla major
A slow growing deciduous shrub related to witch hazel with spikes of feathery white *fls* appearing April, May. *Lvs* like hazel turning spectacular shades of yellows, golds, and orange in autumn. Requires a neutral or lime free soil.

Euonymus alatus
One of the best of all deciduous shrubs for richness in autumn colour. Slow growing deciduous low-spreading shrub to 1.2m/4ft having curious corky wings on shoots. Most soils even shallow chalk.

Hedges

From earliest times when man first settled in communities he realised the need for privacy and shelter. To achieve this requirement he built stone partitions or walls to separate him from his neighbours. Today the basic reasons for planting a hedge remain very much the same. A sense of privacy within our own home and garden is something to treasure, an escape or perhaps a hideaway from the pressures of modern life. Hedges therefore provide a certain degree of seclusion from other people, also they create a natural backcloth to a garden border of shrubs or herbaceous plants.

Aesthetically where screening is required they are far more pleasing to the eye than a solid wall or unnatural fencing, and certainly more economic to establish. Other benefits include protection from neighbouring children or invading animals. Always choose a suitable thorny subject like *Berberis* for maximum protection. Shelter by forming a screen affords protection of a different kind. Particularly in windswept coastal areas hedges reduce the force of the elements and allow a wider range of plants to be grown in the sheltered garden. Perhaps the most obvious aspect of choosing a hedge is remembering that although its major function is screening, with care in selection it can be beautiful, colourful and attractive, through flowers, foliage or fruit.

Types
The initial major division is in the evergreen types which provide all year round protection,

A hedge like this one is fun to own
but hard work to create

A hedge provides many things: beauty, privacy, safety,
and a wide choice of colours whether you want green
all the year round, flowers as well, or fruits. Regular
clipping will keep it healthy and looking good

and the deciduous subjects shedding their leaves in autumn allowing greater wind flow through the hedge. Either type can be used successfully for the second major group, this concerns formal, and informal hedges. Formal hedges are more typically seen in larger, landscaped gardens where internal screens are used to seggregate smaller area. Generally they require maintenance on a regular basis and must be clipped or shaped twice yearly. Plants suited to this system include *Buxus* (Box), *Ilex* (Holly) and *Taxus* (Yew) all evergreens, and among the deciduous types *Carpinus* (Hornbeam) and *Fagus* (Beech). Beech and yew are both ideally suited to chalky soils.

Site Preparation
Cultivation must commence in autumn with double digging and the incorporation of organic manure. All perennial weeds must be eradicated before planting commences and soils allowed to weather during winter.

Planting
The majority of bare rooted subjects should be planted from October to March similar to the trees. It is however possible to plant evergreens slightly later during April and May. Container grown plants extend the season right through summer provided they are well irrigated after planting. The principles of planting are similar to that of the tree, a large enough hole, the addition of peat, firmness of planting, correct depth, and watering after planting.

Spacing
Plant spacing obviously determines how rapidly the hedge will link and join to form a barrier. Distances will vary according to species and growth rate of a particular subject. As a general guide slower subjects should be planted 38–45cm/15–18in apart while the more vigorous subjects, Conifers and large broad leaved evergreens require 75–100cm/30–40in between them.

Maintenance
During the first 2–3 years newly planted hedges

Using shears to trim a hedge

Take plenty of care with an electric hedge trimmer

must be maintained and cared for. Mulching with peat or leaf mould does much to reduce weed populations, if weeds do appear hoeing should eliminate these. Irrigation is also vital to assist establishment particularly in hot dry seasons. Early clipping should be aimed at shaping the hedge rather than drastic cutting. This is carried out using secateurs for large leaved subjects or hand shears for smaller plants. Only when the hedge has reached the desired height should the top be removed. The operation naturally encourages more lateral shoot development and a thicker hedge. As the hedge develops training will determine the type of hedge produced. In general it is wise to keep it broad at the base and taper it to a narrow top. Yew and box lend themselves to this type of management, which often produces strange shapes as seen in the art of topiary.

Where hedges have shown reluctance to produce noticeable new growth an annual dressing of a compound fertilizer may prove beneficial. This technique is often used to stimulate old neglected hedges.

A well-kept hedge the right size for a small front garden

Plant Selection

Evergreens

Aucuba japonica
Hardy, pollution tolerant shrub to 2m/6ft, tolerates sun or shade, most soils. Female plants with red berries, *lvs* yellow spotted green.

Berberis stenophylla
A rather loose spiny hedge. *Fls* orange-yellow April. Berries blue-black. Shoots thorny with short thin leathery *lvs*. Most conditions and soils. Height 2–3m/6–10ft.

Common Box *(Buxus sempervirens)*
Small slow growing, bushy shade-loving ever-greens. Tolerates regular clipping twice yearly and thrives on shallow chalk soils. Many good yellow and variegated forms available. 1m/3ft.

Holly *(Ilex aquifolium)*
Hardy, long-lived pollution resistant slow grow-ing evergreen. *Lvs* deep green leathery with spines. *Fls* white insignificant, berries red round. 6m/20ft.

Deciduous Types

Cotoneaster simonsii
A slow growing upright shrub. *Fls* white in summer, berries red in winter, *lvs* turning rich red in autumn. Bees attracted by flowers. Height 1.5m/6ft.

Golden Bells (*Forsythia intermedia*)
Sturdy early spring flowering shrub, *fls* yellow in March before *lvs*. Prune after flowering April. Will reach 2m/6ft in 3–4 years.

Hornbeam (*Carpinus betulus*)
Tough upright deciduous hedge, buds long pointed, *lvs* veined bright green, autumn brown hanging on ultil spring. 3m/10ft tall.

Hydrangea macrophylla
Excellent summer flowering shrub for milder coastal areas where it is widely used. *Fls* from pink through to blue in conspicuous round heads. Plant March, April in sunny situation.

Conifers

Lawson Cypress (*Chamaecyparis lawsoniana*)
Useful hardy subject for colder areas where taller screens are required. Most exhibit a characteristic concial habit and show a very wide range of foliage colours among the cultivars and varieties. 12m/40ft.

Monterey Cypress (*Cupressus macrocarpa*)
A very quick growing subject exceptionally useful in coastal areas. Tolerates strong salt laden winds. Subject to frost damage when young especially northern areas. Various selections of yellows and golds available.

Leyland Cypress (*Cupressocyparis leylandii*)
Reputed to be fastest growing of all conifers – 1m/3ft per season. Very quick shelter from 2m/6ft spacing will reach 15m/50ft in 15–18 years. The only disadvantage is the shallow root system which may lead to 'wind blow' on shallow soils. A recent introduction equally as fast growing and hardy is the yellow form *C.L.* 'Castlewellan' found in Ireland, now much sought after.

Yew (*Taxus baccata*)
Easily the best conifer for formal hedging. Slow growing, long lasting, tolerant of chalk soils, regular clipping. Only problem is the foliage is poisonous to cattle, and the seed is also poisonous. Height 3m/10ft.

12 The Rock Garden

Building a Rock Garden

Siting

A flourishing rock garden gives tremendous interest. In nature, rock plants thrive where the soil drains sharply; where they are exposed to the full rays of the sun; where they are blanketed by snow in winter. It may not be possible to reproduce these conditions exactly, but we must do what we can. Ideally, site it away from the drips of overhanging trees and shrubs. Put it where it won't be shaded for a large part of the day and where the soil doesn't collect water after a heavy spell of rain. A naturally sloping site is preferable to a level one, but a 'table' rock garden can have great charm. If the ground faces south or south-west, so much the better. A rock garden can be as large or as small as you like, but don't make the mistake of building it with very small pieces of rock. These look absurd and do not give the impression of arising from a solid base. Let's imagine we are constructing one in a sunny part of the garden, sloping down to the lawn. Start by outlining the area with string and canes. If the soil needs draining, remove the top layer and put it on one side for later use, then replace the sticky, badly drained subsoil by a 38cm/15in layer of broken rubble or some other material. Cover the rubble with a single layer of turves, grass side downwards, to stop the soil that you add later from washing through into the drainage material. Make sure the rock garden is not overshadowed by more dominant features such as a shrub border, garden shed or rose arbour: it must command attention.

Construction

It's tremendous fun recreating in miniature a mountain valley, an upthrusting spur, a winding, tubling stream, an alpine lawn, a flower-decked ravine. But whatever you decide to tackle, it must look right. Lumps of stone placed willy nilly look hideous.

If possible, use locally quarried stone. It not only looks more natural but is a lot cheaper than stone which has to be dug a long distance away. Sandstone and limestone mellow quickly and look well. Granite, being very hard, retains a raw harsh look for many years.

If possible, pre-shape the rock garden first. Mould the pockets (tiers), spurs, valleys and scarp faces with soil before you lay a single rock. Then you'll have a good idea what the end result will be. If you've never laid rocks before, and cannot conceive what that heap of stone will look like, make a model of the garden in bits of polystyrene. Glue the pieces together and the effect is realistic. Some rocks can weigh a hundredweight or more, so get a friend to help you manoeuvre them into position. Tool? You will need a spade, fork and a rammer made from a bulk of wood 10cm/4in square 150cm/5ft handle.

Start at the foot of the rock garden. Place a shapely stone in position. This key stone should be tilted backwards slightly. Then it will resemble a rocky outcrop. Sink it one third deep in the soil and ram more soil round so it doesn't wobble. It must be 'rock firm'. Then continue with loop or L-shaped tiers of rock, each one slightly higher than the one before. If you're uncertain how to achieve this, take a look at a

Above: a rockery should be constructed so as to look natural
Left: rock plants will grow on a dry stone wall

rock garden at a botanic garden or, if you live in a hilly or mountainous district, at a naturally eroded bit of mountainside. You will soon see how to achieve a realistic setting.

Each rock has lines running through it—the strata. Make sure that you align the strata; don't have some rocks with their strata running horizontally, others vertically. In nature, the strata of an outcrop are always consistent.

When all the rocks have been placed, well rammed into position, and all sloping backwards slightly so that rain washes the soil back into the pockets rather than away from them, leave the soil and rocks to settle for a fortnight or so before planting.

Planting
You will have chosen dwarf shrubs to punctuate the rock garden; cascaders such as alyssum, aubrietias and saponaria to flow over the outcrops; cushion saxifrages and others to contrast with the trailers and grow over the flat tops of rocks; and some bulbs such as cyclamen to grow up through the carpeters. Start by planting the shrubs. Set dwarf conifers at the base of large rocks and umbrella or mushroom forms to spread over higher promontaries.

Rosette forming ramondas and lewisias hate getting their leaves wet, so plant them with their roots tucked into a vertical fissure. No matter what you plant, so make sure that the roots are well spread out and covered with a good depth of soil.

Watering
In their natural state, rock plants are watered and fed continuously by nutrients dissolved in water derived from melting snow, but because the soil is rocky the roots are never waterlogged. We can reproduce this situation by burying a perforated hosepipe in the garden when we are building it. One end of the pipe is left sticking out and connected to the tap, or another length of pipe, if the tap is some distance away. Then it is possible to supply water at roots level where the plants need it. None is wasted and no soil is washed away.

It also pays to surround rock plants, specially the damp-sensitive, woolly leaved kinds that can rot if too much water gets on to their leaves, specially in winter, with a layer of fine chippings to discourage slugs and wet soil in direct contact with the necks of the plants.

For some odd reason, many people think that rock plants do not need feeding. They do, just like any other garden plants. The best way is to sprinkle a long term fertilizer such as bone meal, round their roots in spring. This will last the whole season, to nourish growth to perfection.

A–Z of Rock Plants

Acaha microphylla (New Zealand burr)
Rapid and invasic carpeter with small bronzy leaves. In summer, mats dotted with arresting short-stemmed crimson spined burrs. Good ground-cover for bulbs. Prostrate.

Achillea chrysocoma
Rosettes of ferny grey green leaves, 10cm/4in high, spreading to 25cm/10in, form attractive woolly carpet. Mustard yellow flowers, 5–8cm/2–3in wide, appear in June and July.

Adonis vernalis
Bright green ferny leaved plant, 23–30cm/9–12in high. In March, butter yellow, cup shaped flowers form on 23cm/9in stems. Plant where no opposition from neighbouring plants.

Ajuga reptans variegate (bugle)
Light blue spikes of flower in spring. Green and silver variegated leaves, good for carpeting in light shade.

Aethionema coridifolium 'Warley Rose'
Thrives in hot dry positions. 10cm/4in high, spreading. From May to July plants covered with rose-pink daphne-like flowers. Good for limy soil.

Alyssum saxatile
Superb cascader massed with lemon or mustard yellow flowers in spring. Vigorous, so plant where it won't smother slower growers.

Anchusa caespitosa
Valued for its hummocks of narrow dark green leaves and tufts of gentian blue flowers in May to July. 5–8cm/2–3in high, 15cm/6in across. Full sun.

Aquilegia ecalcarata (columbine)
Reddish purple 'granny's bonnet' flowers on lightly branching stems, 23–30cm/9–12in high. Full sun. Leaves finely cut and attractive.

Stonecrop (saxifrage) is good for rock gardens or sink gardens

Arabis albida 'Flore Pleno'
Massed with white flowers from February to June. Non-invasive clumps, full sun. Good for walls, paving or screes. Soft green leaves.

Armeria maritima (thrift)
Cushions of tight narrow leaves give rise to vivid rose pink flowers, like pom-poms, on 15cm/6in stems, from May to July. Full sun. Good seaside plant.

Artemisia stelleriana
Superb bright silvery ferny leaves. Excellent for edging or planting in pockets close to deep green leaved plants. Protect in winter from rain by covering with pane of glass.

Arum italicum 'Pictum'
Arrow-shaped glossy green leaves marbled with white. In autumn, spikes of close set scarlet berries. Needs cool soil, 23cm/9in high, 38cm/15in across.

Aster alpinus 'Beechwood'
Mauve-blue daisy flowers, 3cm/1½in across, on 23cm/9in stems. Spread, 38–45cm/15–18in, July. Best in full sun.

Astilbe chinensis 'Pumila'
Spikes of rose-purple, foam-like flowers, 23–30cm/9–12in high, in August. Spread, 30cm/12in. Ferny leaves. Prefers cool, moist soil.

Aubrieta
Cascading or mat forming spring flowerer with bright rose-red, purple, blue or mauve blooms that literally smother the plant. Any soil, full sun.

Bellis perennis 'Dresden China'
The double pink-flowered ornamental daisy, 8cm/3in high, 15cm/6in across. Divide regularly to maintain vigour. Summer flowering.

Berberis thunbergii 'Atropurpurea Nana'
Superb purple-leaved form rarely growing more than 45cm/18in high and 60cm/24in across. Excellent feature shrub.

Campanula carpatica
Large starry cup-shaped flowers in blue, purple or white, in June to August. Clump-forming, 23cm/9in high, 38cm/15in across. Full sun.

Cyclamen neapolitanum
15cm/6in stems topped with pale pink to rich rose blooms; autumn. Rounded marbled leaves.

Good for naturalizing in light shade. Peaty, gritty soil.

Daphne cneorum
Dwarf evergreen shrub 60–90cm/24–30in high and across, clusters of richly scented, deep pink flowers from May to June. Excellent as a feature.

Dianthus deltoides (maiden pink)
Innumerable crimson flowers 15–23cm/6–9in high on clumps 30cm/12in across, from June to September. Grow where plants can arch over rocky outcrop.

Dicentra formosa
Arching stems wreathed with deep pink locket-shaped flowers. Leaves thick and ferny, good for ground cover. Blooms appear in May and June. Plants 38cm/15in high and 45cm/18in across.

Erodium chamaedryoides (stork's bill)
Rosettes of ferny leaves give rise to 8–10cm/3–4in high stems topped with bright

Above: miniature daffodils shown off to advantage on a rockery
Left: anemones will grow well among rocks

Gentians bring a splash of colour to the rock garden

rose-red flowers all summer long. Spread, about 23cm/9in.

Euryops acraeus
Handsome silver leaved bush 30cm/12in high and across, massed with bright yellow flowers in summer. Clip hard when leggy to retain its shapeliness.

Fuchsia 'Tom Thumb'
Summer and late summer flowering variety with large rose-scarlet and violet ballet-skirted blooms massed on stems 30cm/12in high and across.

Genista lydia
Arching stems set with close packed small leaves, decked with golden pea flowers from May to June. 60cm/24in high, 90cm/36in across. One of the finest shrubs for a rock garden. Set where can be admired by all. Full sun.

Gentiana sino-ornata
Vivid blue trumpets from September to October. 15cm/6in high, 30cm/12in across. Forms sheets of foliage. Needs a lime-free soil, easy.

Geranium dalmaticum
Large rounded clear pink flowers 2.5cm/1in across on stems 10cm/4in high; spread 23cm/9in. Glossy rounded leaves assume bright coppery red tints in autumn. Flowers appear from June to August.

Gypsophila fratensis
Creeping plant smothered with soft pink flowers in June. Prostrate; spread, 38cm/15in. Best in full sun on sharply draining soil.

Helianthemum nummularium (rock rose).
Cushions of small evergreen leaves massed with yellow, red, pink hued flowers from June to July. 15cm/6in high, 60cm/24in across. Full sun.

Leontopodium alpinum (edelweiss)
Silver grey felted spidery flowers on 15–23cm/6–9in stems. Leaves silvery grey, also felted. Blooms from June to July. Spread, 23cm/9in.

Oenothera missouriensis (evening primrose)
Impressive glossy yellow cup-shaped flowers 5cm/2in across, borne on trailing stems from June to August. 10–15cm/4–6in high, 45cm/18in across.

Oxalis adenophylla
Valued for its clusters of pink trumpet flowers from May to July. Handsome foliage, like shamrock. Height, 8cm/3in, spread, 15cm/6in.

Phlox subulata
Prostrate spreading mats covered with fiery crimson, apple-blossom pink, moonlight-blue or white flowers from April to May. 5cm/2in high, 45cm/18in across.

If your garden has no place for a rockery, try a sink
garden

Primulas give spring colour to the rock garden

Primula auricula

Impressive heads of bloom in yellow and purple shades, often with a distinctive white eye. Evergreen leaves milky green. Flowers from March to May. Height 23cm/9in, spread 38cm/15in.

Saxifraga longifolia 'Tumbling Waters'

A real treasure. Rosettes of narrow leaves give rise to immense, often 60cm/24in long, arching sprays of pure white flowers. Flowers June to August.

Sedum floriferum 'Weihenstephaner Gold'

Spreading, prostrate plant decked with 8cm/3in high stems of golden yellow starry flowers in August. Leaves thick and fleshy.

Sempervivum (houseleek)

Large family. One of the best is S. 'Commander Hay', whose fleshy, spine tipped leaf rosettes turn a pretty reddish hue in autumn and winter. Best for scree gardens.

Solidago brachystachys (golden rod)

Splendid miniature form with dense spikes of golden flowers coming in usefully in autumn when few other plants are in bloom. Height 15cm/6in, spread 38cm/15in. Thin narrow leaves of little garden value.

Thymus serpyllum (thyme)

Aromatic flowering carpeter with pink and red shades of bloom. Flowers mass the soft woolly cushions from June to August. Beloved by bees.

Viola cornuta (horned pansey)

Delicate spurred viola-like blooms in blue or white appear in June and July. Height 15cm/6in, spread 38cm/15in. Excellent ground cover.

Zauscheria california 'Mexicana'

Loose stems of bright red foxglove-like flowers bloom in September and October to give the rock garden a final splash of colour. 30–38cm/12–15in high and 60cm/24in across.

13 Water in the Garden – Ponds and Pools

Making a Garden Pool

Richly hued waterlilies, reflections on a still, warm summer's day, the plop of an eager goldfish as it surfaces to snap at a careless fly–such are some of the attractions of a garden pool. It is easy to make, can be completed in a day and will bring a lifetime's interest. It can be of any shape, though one which fits in harmoniously with the surroundings is preferable.

Construction

Site it in full sun and well away from shrubs and overhanging trees whose leaves would blow into and foul the water. Unless you are using a pre-shaped fibreglass pool, which is simply sunk rim level into a suitably sized hole, you will need to dig out the shape you require. A rectangle, square or circle is best if the surroundings are for nal, but an irregular, say kidney shape, is more in keeping with an informal area. Whether small or large in size, it should be between 38cm/15in and 60cm/24in deep, otherwise it will heat up too much in summer and suffer from a lack of oxygen; in winter, there may be more ice in proportion to water, and again the fish would suffer. Slope the sides of the pool gently and cut out shelves in the soil, about 23cm/9in below the rim, to house marginal plants which are only covered with a few inches of water.

When the excavation is complete, line the bottom and sides with soft sand to cover any sharp stones which might otherwise puncture the liner, be it butyl rubber, plastic in the form of polythene or PVC, or PVC reinforced with nylon mesh.

Lay the liner in the pool and ease out all the wrinkles you can. Then Tension the sides by placing flat stones, paving or bricks around the edge. When you're absolutely satisfied that not a stone can bore into the material and that there is a good foot of material overlapping the edge of the pool, fill in with water from a hosepipe.

Finally, trim the edges of the material to leave a generous overlap, then cover this with 45cm/18in sq paving slabs set firmly in place with mortar. The slabs should project slightly over the edge of the pool to hide the liner and present a pleasing finish.

A fountain adds great charm, oxygenates the water and the sound of tinkling water on a warm June day is extremely relaxing. Most kinds are easily fitted and an Otter submersible pump will ensure a satisfying spray of water.

Planting the Pool

Allow the water to settle for a week or two before introducing plants. This ensures that any harmful minerals in the water are neutralized. If the water turns green, don't worry. This is perfectly normal. Don't attempt to empty and refill the pool–the water will only turn green again. The greenness is algae proliferating in the unshaded water. When aquatic plants shade the pool, the green algae will die out and the water will become crystal clear.

The Plants you Need

To create interest for much of the year set the 23cm/9in shelf round the edge with marginal plants such as green, pink and cream-leaved *Acorus calamus,* golden flowered marsh marigolds and irises in many beautiful lavender and pinkish red shades. Plant them in small slatted plastic baskets.

Then you will need some oxygenating plants which help to keep the water pure and the fish, snails and other water animals healthy. Oxygenators are usually bought in bunches and are fixed to a lump of lead or a stone, with a rubber band and plopped into the pool where they will start growing regardless of soil. These plants also stop the water from turning green and cloudy and provide the ideal spawning ground for fish.

The different kinds include water thyme (elodea), water milfoil *(Myriophyllum spicatum)* and pondweed *(Potamogeton crispum)*.

Floating plants such as water lilies and the water violet *(Aponogeton distachyum)* give a pool that luxuriant look in summer when their chalice like blooms in many colours shine excitingly in the water.

Planting Methods

Marginals and water lilies are best set in wickerwork or slatted plastic baskets. Pack their roots round with heavy, almost clayey soil. Never use manure, or this will discolour the water. Add a sachet of aquatic plant fertilizer, and top the soil with fine shingle to stop fish nosing it into the water and clouding it. Set a newly planted water lily with its leaves just above the water surface. Lower it gradually as the leaves grow, until finally it is resting on the floor of the pool, with its extended leaves floating gracefully on the surface.

Calculating the Area of a Pool

To ascertain how much liner you will need for your pool, the length will be the length of the pool plus twice the maximum depth, and the width will be the width of the pool plus twice the maximum depth.

Materials

Years ago, before plastics were developed, concrete was used to construct a pool. Some people are still keen on using it, saying that it outlasts other materials. It can last for many years, but does have a tendency to develop hairline cracks. These are difficult to find. If the water level drops to a dangerous level, and you suspect such fractures, drain the pool, clean the concrete and paint the whole of the inside with Pondseal. If you're keen on making a concrete liner this is what you do: Dig out the shape you want, ram rubble or stones into the base, then spread a 8cm/3in thickness of concrete over the excavated area. A good mix consists of 1 part cement, 1 part sharp sand and 5 parts sea shingle. Allow the first layer almost to set, then score it with the point of a trowel. A day or so later, spread this layer with a further 8cm/3in thickness of concrete. Fill in with water after 24 hours, then change the water four or five times before planting and introducing the fish.

Other Materials

Polythene Probably the cheapest on the market. 500 gauge usually used. Ideally lay two sheets to increase durability, and make sure it is completely covered with water to reduce the effect of ultra violet light, which causes it to become brittle and crack.

PVC More expensive than polythene; only a single sheet required. It has a greater resistance than polythene to ultra violet light deterioration.

PVC reinforced with nylon mesh This double laminated material is tough and durable and has a much longer life than both polythene and ordinary PVC.

Butyl rubber Specially toughened rubber sheeting with a very long life. It is unaffected by weather and ultra violet light and doesn't wrinkle up so much as polythene or PVC.

Fibreglass Sold as moulded containers, complete with shelves for marginal plants. Very durable, light to handle. Simply dig a hole and sink a fibreglass pool to its rim. Alternatively, dig a shallow hole, then pack the excavated soil up round the pool and build a rock garden round it. Then you have a rock garden with a water garden as a centrepiece.

Right: a formal water garden
Below: no pond is complete without
water lilies

A–Z of Pond Plants

Marginals (those grown on the shelf around the inside edge of the pool and covered with just a few inches of water)

Acorus calamus variegatus (sweet flag)
Leaves striped brightly with green, pink and cream, 60cm/24in high. Yellow flowers, June to July.

Alisma plantago (water plantain)
Branching spikes of rose pink small flowers from June to August. 30–60cm/12–24in high. Leaves long and tapering.

Caltha palustris 'Plena' (double marsh marigold)
Spreading hummocks of glossy rounded leaves set with short branching flower stalks topped with dense pom-poms of bright golden yellow flowers from April to June. Height 30–38cm/12–15in.

Cyperus longus (sweet galingale)
Attractive sedge with chestnut brown plumes of bloom from July to September. Height, 90cm/36in.

Iris kaempferi 'Higo Strain' (clematis flowered iris)
Sumptuous reddish purple violet, blue or white extra large blooms from July to August. Height, 60–90cm/24–36in.

Mimulus luteus (monkey musk)
Yellow, maroon blotched pouch-like flowers from May to August. Rampant spreader; needs plenty of room. 20–45cm/8–18in high.

Myosotis palustris (water-forget-me-not)
Delicate sprays of intense blue flowers from June to August. Height, 23–30cm/9–12in.

Orontium aquaticum (golden club)
Impressive spikes of yellow club-like petalless flowers appear in from May to June. Height, 15–30cm/6–12in. Will either float or become a free-standing plant.

Pontederia cordata (pickeral weed)
Spikes of arresting purple-blue flowers from August to September. Attractive shining dark green oval leaves. Height, 50–75cm/20–30in.

Sagittaria sagittifolia (arrowhead)
Grown for its imposing arrow head shaped leaves and stiffish spikes of white flowers. A double form is particularly impressive. Height 38–45cm/15–18in.

Oxygenators (submerged plants which keep the water charged with oxygen to ensure a healthy balance of floating and marginal plants, and fish).

Ceratophyllum demersum (hornwort)
Attractive whorls of rather brittle, green leaves, so handle with care when planting it.

Elodea crispa (curled Canadian pondweed)
Stems clothed with downwards curving leaves.

Fontinalis antipyretica (willow moss)
Masses of soft feathery foliage.

Myriophyllum spicatum (water milfoil)
Lengthy stems set with candelabras of soft finely dissected leaves.

Potamogeton crispum (curled pondweed)
Beautiful long thin, wavy edged leaves bright green to bronzy purple in colour.

Free Floating Aquatics
Azolla caroliniana (fairy floating moss)
Spreads to form a reddish green carpet of delicate fingered ferny growths. Ideal for shading the water to reduce the growth of water greening algae.

Hydrocharis morsus-ranae (frogbit)
Charming small white flowers appear surrounded by tiny rounded waterlily-like leaves in June and July.

Caring for the Garden Pool

A well balanced community of fish and snails and floating, oxygenating and marginal plants requires little attention to maintain it as a superb garden feature.

Points to note:
Green soupy water a week or so after filling a

Above: a formal pool
Right: a formal water avenue

Above: a tiny pond
Right: a natural water feature is a great advantage

A raised water garden

new pool with tap water is due to algae feeding on the temporarily salts enriched liquid. Do not attempt to clear the water by draining and refilling. The algae will disappear when a perfect balance of fish and plants is achieved, and when the water is lightly shaded by floating plants.

Blanket weed is a form of long stringy algae which can build up in the presence of sunlight. If it reaches choking proportions, remove what you can by entwining it round the working head of a rake.

Use an algae killer if the water stays green, despite your efforts to cleanse it by shading it with plants. Algimycin is an effective algicide. Use it according to manufacturer's instructions. You will need to know the cubic capacity and number of gallons your pool holds. This is calculated simply by multiplying length by breadth by the average depth. The answer is the cu ft your pool contains. If then you multiply

this number by $6\frac{1}{4}$ (the number of gallons in a cu ft of water) you will arrive at the gallonage of your pool.

Spring clean your pool by cutting off dead and yellowing leaves from water lilies and marginal plants. Replant in good heavy soil marginals and lilies that have outgrown their baskets, obviously using a larger sized container. This is also a good time to divide large clumps of plants and either replant them, setting them elsewhere in the pool, or give them to your friends. April, May and June are the best months for this.

In autumn, spread a fine net over the pool surface to stop leaves falling into and fouling the water.

In winter, stop ice forming over the entire surface by leaving a rubber ball in the water. It is important to keep a hole in the ice to allow gases from decomposing vegetation to escape and not build up to endanger the fish. And never break the ice by pounding it with a hammer. The shock waves set up can harm the fish.

If you suspect herons of taking your fish, the only cure is to stretch a net over water, and to keep it there.

If the side of your pool is paved, check that the slabs are firmly fixed to their bed of mortar. If they are loose and liable to tip forward set them in fresh mortar when the weather is mild and not liable to be frosty.

Cats have a habit of lurking beside a pool and deftly flicking fish from the water. If you discover your fish are being angled in this fashion, either use a cat repellant or plant low prickly shrubs round the edge of the pool.

Water Lilies
Without them, their vivid colours and exotic pad-like leaves, a garden pool would lose much of its charm. There are large, medium and small kinds for pools from 10–90cm/4–36in deep. Take your pick from the followig hardy kinds.

For water 10–25cm/4–10in deep, there is white pygmaea alba, pink laydekeri lilacea, red pygmaea rubra and yellow and orange pygmaea helvola.

For water from 25–40cm/10–16in deep, there is

white Albatross, pink Rose Arey, red Froebeli and orange yellow flushed coppery pink Graziella.

For water from 40–50cm/16–20in deep, there is white marlicea albida, pink Firecrest, red James Brydon and sulphur yellow Moorei.

For water 50–90cm/20–36in deep there is white gladstoniana, pink Mrs. Richmond, red Escarboucle and canary yellow Col. Welch.

Water lilies are best planted in slatted plastic buckets of heavy soil top with stone chippings.

Fish

What grace and beauty they lend to the pool. How hypnotic their effortless glides among the lilies. Goldfish, shubunkins and a green tench or two to act as scavengers, really bring the water to life. Wait a few weeks after planting the floaters and oxygenators before introducing the fish. Then they will feel at home in a pool that has had a chance to grow a little algae round the sides for them to feed upon, and to attract perhaps gnat larvae, those black wrigglers that the fish love to eat.

How many fish will fit comfortably into your pool? Allow one per 30cm^2/12in^2 of surface area. Don't over-feed them. In fact, there is no necessity to feed them at all, but it is nice to see them gather round to a side of the pool once a day when you bring them food, and this is a habit that both you and the fish are keen on cultivating.

Don't feed the fish from November to March, as their systems are sluggish and the water is too cold for them to digest their food properly. Should one become covered in saprolegnia fungus, a cotton wool like disease, isolate it from the rest and try to kill the disease with a little salt water, or consult your nearest aquarist.

Above: even a tub can be made into a water garden – it must be lined
Right: there are many different kinds of water lily

14 Greenhouses and Frames

Types of Greenhouse and Frame

Today gardeners are fortunate in being able to choose from a wide range of greenhouse shapes and materials of construction. It is wise to choose the largest you can afford or find a place for in the garden. Alternatively, select one that can be extended any time more space is required. Both frames and greenhouses are usually now made from weather resistant timbers, such as cedar, galvanized steel, or aluminium alloy. They are easy to erect in a short time with screws or nuts and bolts, and usually without professional assistance. However, when a greenhouse is erected on a base wall of brick, it is better to obtain the services of a skilled brick-layer.

It is wise to take aluminium alloy first into consideration. It can also be obtained with white or green plastic coating. Aluminium is virtually everlasting and needs no painting. It will not warp, corrode, rot, or become attacked by wood-boring insects. It is lightweight, and most structures are easily taken down if it is desired at any time to change your site or home. Galvanized steel is extremely strong, but it does need painting from time to time. If the zinc covering is damaged rust may set in. All metal frames lend themselves to simple glazing using clips instead of putty. In some cases metal frames may be thought too harsh for a garden. The mellow appearance of timber may be thought to blend better. The most popular timber is red cedar which is attractive and relatively inexpensive as well as having a good weather resistance.

Frames are usually square or rectangular, but types with a good slope to the 'light' (the lid that's raised) should be chosen. This is to ensure run-off of condensation. Greenhouses are available with six or more sides to give a circular shape, but the square or rectangular and 'barn' type shapes are still the best for practical purposes. However, hexagonal or other roundish shapes often make pleasingly attractive greenhouses for ornamental plants and to use as garden features or on a patio.

Some greenhouses have the glass set at an angle so as to give sloping sides. This is to let the maximum sunlight in during the winter months when the sun is low in the sky. If the glass is angled there is less thickness to absorb the sun's rays, since glass is not completely transparent. Even so, very sloped sides can be a nuisance when working and make the fitting of staging awkward. For most home greenhouses a slight slope, or vertical sides, will be found more convenient.

Greenhouses with the glass to ground level, or almost so, are the most versatile. If fitted with staging there will be sufficient light underneath to allow some useful growing. Tall plants can be grown from ground level without suffering from lack of light in their early stages. Greenhouses with a low base wall or boarded base (usually called 'plant houses') may keep in warmth better, but the base obstructs sunlight and there may consequently be a loss of free solar warmth. Which is most suited is a matter of individual preference.

The plastics are now used extensively for both frames and greenhouses, but their advantages

Above: a cold frame will be useful if you have a greenhouse
Right: you will appreciate a solid path to a greenhouse

and disadvantages should be understood before choosing. Plastics have a limited life and being soft, they do not weather so well as glass. Glass also has the unique property of trapping solar warmth and retaining it for some time, as well as holding artificial warmth better. On the other hand, the lightweight and unbreakable nature of plastic makes it ideal for where there are children or a frame or greenhouse needs to be moved about on a site, such as for vegetable growing. The most inexpensive plastic house uses polythene. This must be a special grade called UVI which is less affected by the ultra violet light in the sun's rays causing ordinary polythene to quickly become brittle and disintegrate. UVI polythene will last for at least two years. Other more rigid plastics are longer lasting. Novolux corrugated sheeting is said to last at least five years; and structures comparing favourably with glass can be constructed with it. It is excellent for making portable frames. With glass frames the lights are often heavy and susceptible to breakage.

When choosing a greenhouse see that facilities for ventilation are good. A sliding door is also useful as an extra vent. Some frames have sliding sections in the base which allows ventilation without raising the top.

Site

The site for a greenhouse should always be as open and sunny as possible. All plants must have adequate light and it is easy enough to shade when required. Plenty of sun means free heating and even in winter a little sun filtering through the clouds will shoot up the greenhouse temperature. However, many popular decorative and conservatory pot plants prefer shady and cool condition. If it is proposed to grow these only, a shady site, such as a conservatory or lean-to against a north facing wall, may be found suitable. When frames are used in conjunction with the greenhouse, and to take over some of the shorter plants, they too can be sited in some shade. Usually the north side of a greenhouse is convenient. However, a site near trees is to be avoided in all cases. Trees soil the glass or plastic with exuded gums and falling leaves, and also harbour pests and diseases. Small ornamentals are alright at a reasonable distance. A fence or hedge suitably placed may also act as a wind break. A site in a hollow is also to be avoided if possible. It can become waterlogged and a frost pocket in icy weather.

It is useful not to have the greenhouse too far from the dwelling. A lean-to that can be entered from the house is often a delightful place for ornamentals. When the greenhouse is near it is easier to run electricity or even to extend the domestic central heating to the greenhouse. A water tap can be fitted with little trouble.

Basic Equipment

Although much can be done with an unheated greenhouse, its range will be greatly increased by some form of heating–even just enough to keep out frost. The most extensively used heater is the simple paraffin wick type, but it must always be employed in conjunction with some ventilation to allow air in and for any fumes to escape. The same applies to natural gas heaters with no flue. Both these fuels need air for proper combustion. They both evolve considerable water vapour, and unless there is reasonable ventilation this can cause much condensation. Hot water pipes can be used, preferably where higher temperatures are required. The boilers can be heated by solid fuel, paraffin oil, waste car sump oil, fuel oil, or natural gas. Electricity is not recommended in this case, since immersion heaters consume too much electricity. Modern hot water pipe systems are simple to install, and lightweight aluminium pipes have replaced the old very heavy cast iron.

Properly used, electricity is practical and should compare favourably in price with other fuels. This is because it allows extremely accurate thermostatic control and none need be wasted. Most other fuels may seem cheaper, but they can not be consumed to give their theoretical full heat output. The best electrc heaer is the fan type. However, this should have a fan that comes on only with the heat and does not run continuously. A separate rod type thermostat is also preferable to the built-in type, and gives much more accurate control. A little extra spent on a good quality accurate thermostat is a wise investment and will soon recover its cost in lower fuel bills. Electric heating tubes are also reasonably economical on fuel, provided they are not set too near the greenhouse sides. They are best well distributed around the greenhouse and not all banked in one place as is so often seen. Again they should be used in conjunction with an accurate thermostat.

It is of the utmost importance to choose a heater that will cope with severe cold spells and maintain the minimum temperature you require. If a supplier of heating equipment is given the size and type of greenhouse you have, details of constructional materials, and lowest outside temperature expected together with the minimum inside temperature required, an assessment of the heater rating will be made and recommended. The rating is usually in watts for electricity and British Thermal Units per hour for other fuels. Whatever fuel is decided on, it is wise to have a paraffin heater handy in case of breakdowns and, in these days, strikes.

Staging is sold as an extra, but is often useful especially where pot plants are grown. Portable separate staging can be obtained which can be moved about or put up and taken down to suit growing needs. The staging top is best covered with polythene and a layer of grit kept moist for the summer months. This helps to maintain a damp atmosphere which the plants like. In winter, dry conditions are preferable and the covering is best allowed to go dry or taken off altogether. If the staging is topped with slats or wire mesh, a better air circulation will take place during the winter months which helps to keep down fungoid diseases, as well as the circulation of warm air where there is heating. Some shelving is also often useful and if this is easily portable or removable all the better.

Somewhere to do potting is most desirable, and it is a simple matter to make a portable potting bench that can be put on the staging when needed. To do this take a sheet of aluminium and turn up three of the sides to form a tray. On this compost can be mixed and operations like sowing and potting carried out.

Some form of automatic watering is well worth considering. There are several excellent types now sold. The simplest is capillary matting which can be spread on the staging and kept moist by running guttering along the front. The matting is dipped into the gutter which is kept topped up with water by a small constant level water valve.

An essential piece of equipment is a maximum and minimum thermometer. Only with the aid of this can you keep track of the temperatures and check the efficiency of your heating if installed.

Tomatoes

The tomato is undoubtedly the most popular of all greenhouse food crops, and very few home greenhouses are without them. However, a common mistake is to grow them in the ground soil of the greenhouse. This is alright when the house is plastic and can be moved to a different spot on the vegetable garden each year, but not when the house is permanent and the same soil has to be continuously cropped. This is because the tomato soon suffers from 'soil sickness'. On a particular soil a good crop is usually obtained the first year, but afterwards pests and diseases, and other troubles resulting from an over-used soil, soon cause serious deterioration. Some growers like to change the soil each year, but this is laborious, not always effective, and unnecessary. It is far easier and more reliable to grow the plants in pots or other containers such as Grow Bags. The latter are plastic bags filled with a special compost which are put flat on the ground. Holes are cut in the side through which the plants are planted. Ring culture is also popular. In this method bottomless rings made from fibre are set on a layer of peat or grit kept moist with water. The tomato compost is put in the rings, such as John Innes No 3, or any proprietary potting compost, and the plants. Only the rings are given liquid feeds, but should they dry out they must be remoistened with water. If the peat or grit layer is kept constantly moist the compost in the rings should take up water by capillary action. The layer should be spread on polythene sheeting and be about 10–15cm/4–6in thick. The rings are usually about 23–25cm/9–10in in diameter. The theory of this method is that the fine fibrous roots that form at the top of the root system more readily take in liquid feeds, and the basal roots the plant's needs for water. When this method is employed there is less trouble from cracked skins, and flower and young fruit drop, common when small pots are used and moisture conditions at the roots vary widely between dry and wet.

The plants should be trained up strings or canes by twining them around the support in a clockwise direction. All shoots, except those carrying flower buds, that form where leaves join the main stem must be removed as soon as this can be done without damage. When cropping the temperature of the greenhouse must be kept preferably below about 27°C/80°F or the red pigment in the fruits will not form properly. There will then be trouble from 'greenback' and blotchy ripening. To aid pollination and a good fruit set, spray the flowers with a fine mist of water each morning preferably when conditions are bright and warm. For shading use a *white* shading paint on the outside glass, such as Coolglass. Heavy shading and green shading should be avoided. It is easy to raise your own plants from seed. This also allows a wide selection of varieties which the leading seedsmen describe in their catalogues. A firm favourite for general purposes is Alicante.

Chrysanthemums

Late flowering chrysanthemums are splendid as a follow up for tomatoes, since whilst the tomatoes are cropping they can be grown on outside. They need greenhouse protection only from autumn onwards. There are very many different chrysanthemum types and they may bear numerous small flowers or a few extremely large ones. Most greenhouse types need training like stopping and disbudding. These operations are not difficult and a catalogue from any leading specialist will give full explanation. A catalogue is a further essential, because the stopping times can vary with each variety. The stopping and disbudding is done to obtain the best quality flowers at the right time.

The plants are sold as rooted cuttings and they should be potted up from February to March using 13–15cm/5–6in pots of John Innes No 3 compost. At first the plants can be kept in a frost free greenhouse or frame. By June the plants can be given 20–23cm/8–9in pots and stood out in the open. Choose a place sheltered from wind, but take precautions to see they are well secured so that they don't blow over as the plants become sizable. Canes and wires will be needed for support. Keep the plants well watered and fed and transfer to the greenhouse by about mid-September for flowering.

Pot Plants

Cinerarias and calceolarias
These are great old favourites, very showy and colourful from Christmas to spring. Sow from May to June, transfer the seedlings to seed trays, and later to 9cm/$3\frac{1}{2}$in pots. By late summer move on to 13cm/5in or larger pots for flowering. Keep a special watch for aphids.

Schizanthus and salpiglossis
Two more very showy and easy plants. Sow in autumn and grow on over winter in a frost free house for spring display. Pot on as the plants grow. Pinch out the growing tip of salpiglossis when the seedlings are about 8cm/3in tall. Similarly treat schizanthus, but make further stopping to side shoots to induce bushy growth. Give at least 13cm/5in pots for flowering.

Primulas
There are several charming species. Sow in May for plants flowering from early winter onwards. Pot on to 13cm/5in pots for flowering. Water preferably with *clean* rainwater, since these plants do not like hard or limey water. Polyanthus, of the same family, may be treated similarly but are best sown from February to March. A frost free frame makes good accommodation. It should be slightly shaded.

Fuchsia
Everyone seems to like these distinctive flowers. Buy from a specialist nursery preferably obtaining rooted cuttings in early spring. Give 13cm/5in pots or larger as needed and keep slightly shaded in a frost free greenhouse. There are many types suited for baskets or to grow as bush form or to train as standards. Nursery catalogues give training hints.

Pelargoniums
These include what are popularly called 'geraniums' and there are also scented foliage types. Again choose from a specialist nursery. Show or Regal pelargoniums are usually kept in the greenhouse since they are more liable to weather damage. They have numerous very showy flowers. All pelargoniums should be carefully watered so that they are not waterlogged, and they mostly like bright conditions, the Regals tolerating more shade. Excellent 'geraniums' can now be raised from Fl hybrid seed.

Begonias
Named varieties of show begonias are expensive but the most impressive. It is wise to begin with cheaper tubers. Start them into growth in warmth in spring and transfer to 13cm/5in pots. Support with a cane and keep compost moist and the house shaded and humid. There are also many foliage types with very decorative foliage. These are best bought as young plants.

Cyclamen
Popular but not one of the easiest greenhouse plants. Beginners would be advised to start from corms which can be started into growth from July to August. Seed can be sown from September to November, but needs a steady temperature of about 15°C/60°F minimum for best results. Cooler conditions can be given during flowering which usually takes about ten months from seed.

Coleus
This indispensable foliage plant is one of the most exciting and colourful there is, yet simple to raise from seed. Sow in early spring transferring the seedlings to trays until the leaf colours can be seen and selected for potting. There are several new forms with fancy foliage and unusual colouring. Give final 13cm/5in pots. It is not worth keeping the plants over winter, since they need considerable warmth then.

Right: begonias

Right: chionodoxa in a pot
Far right: freesias are quite easy to grow

Cucumbers

These can now be grown in company with tomatoes. New F1 hybrids are vigorous and new pesticides can be used on both crops without damage. There are all female varieties that do not produce male flowers which should be normally removed from ordinary varieties each morning to prevent pollination. When this occurs the fruits become club shaped and often bitter and seedy. The male flowers carry no tiny cucumber behind them.

Grow the plants in 25cm/10in pots on the staging and train them up behind wires stretched about 15–20cm/6–8in apart the length of the greenhouse. Tie lateral shoots to these wires as they grow. Stop the plants when the last wire is reached and the laterals about two leaves on from where a fruit forms. Any further laterals that form can be treated similarly. Cucumbers must be watered with discretion. They are frequently given far too much.

Bedding Plants

These are now very profitable greenhouse products since they are expensive in shops. By growing your own you can also benefit from the many exciting new introductions each year. You can also achieve better quality. Sowing can start from January onwards if you have a warm propagator, but quick growing types like African and French marigolds should be left until about April when little artificial warmth is required. Sowing should be in small trays or pans which must be kept moist. A proper seed compost should be used and the sowing done thinly. Prick out the seedlings into trays as soon as they can be handled. Large seeds, of say zinnia, can be sown directly in pots.

It is wise to water in the seedlings with Cheshunt Compound as a routine after pricking out to prevent damping off diseases. All seedlings must be hardened off in frames before planting out when all danger of frost has passed. To do this keep the frame closed all the time at first, then give day ventilation and finally ventilation all the time. This should take about two to three weeks according to the prevailing weather.

15 Grow your Own Vegetables

With the ever increasing cost of vegetables, it makes more sense now than ever before to grow your own. It is not difficult, or even excessively space consuming; you can grow vegetables with attractive foliage among the flowers—carrots, beetroot and runner beans are all good to look at as well as to eat. The important thing is that any vegetable site should have plenty of sunlight, and that you should remember to rotate your crops to keep the soil in good condition and to prevent pests and diseases particular to one group of plants from building up in the earth.

Most people use three rotation groups: the brassicas (cabbage, broccoli, sprouts, cauliflower, kale); legumes (peas and the different kinds of beans); and roots (carrots, beetroot, early potatoes and so on). If you have the time and inclination to grow maincrop potatoes, these will form a fourth group with the earlies included, and your land should be rotated in four sections.

The list below describes the most popular vegetables; if you want to grow more unusual or difficult crops, it will be best to buy a specialist vegetable book.

Beetroot
Seed can be grown from mid-April in the south of England, and from early May in the north. Make drills about 2.5cm/1in deep and leave 50cm/15in between rows. Space the seeds at 8cm/3in intervals, and after they have come up, thin them to 15cm/6in. Make sowings each month until July to ensure a regular supply.

Dig the roots up carefully, as there will be considerable loss of flavour if the skins are broken, and make sure you have them all out of the ground before the first frosts. Good varieties: Avon Early, Detroit Globe, Boltardy.

Broccoli
Seed should be sown in a well dug and raked seedbed, and you must thin them as soon as they are large enough to handle. Transplant the young plants in June, leaving 60cm/24in between them, and making the soil very firm around the bases. Stake the plants if you live in a windy area. The worst pest that attacks broccoli, as all the members of the brassica family, is clubroot; see page 148 for information on control. Varieties: Early Penzance, Royal Oak, Early Purple Sprouting.

Broad Bean
Broad beans like well dug soil, and manure or garden compost will do them a lot of good. In sheltered gardens, sowings can be made in November, otherwise wait until March. Plant the seeds in double rows 20cm/8in apart, with 15cm/6in between the seeds. When the flowers have formed, pinch out the growing tips to discourage blackfly attacks. Taller growing varieties may need some support. Varieties: Aquadulce, The Sutton, The Midget.

Cabbage
Sow seeds in June or July for summer crops the following year, and in March for cabbages the same autumn. Sow thinly in drills 20cm/8in apart, and set the plants out 40cm/16in apart. Pests and diseases are the same as for broccoli. Varieties: Greyhound, Primo, Fillgap.

Nothing tastes better than a well-grown cauliflower

Carrot

Seed should be sown in shallow drills 20cm/8in apart from early April until June for succession. Thin the seedlings out as soon as possible after they have germinated, as this will discourage carrot fly which may otherwise devastate the crop. If you have clay soil, sow stump-rooted varieties. Make sure the tops are not showing above ground during growth as this will make them turn hard and green. Varieties: Chantenay, Early Nantes.

Cauliflower

Sow seed in September in a frame or under cloches for an early summer crop, or sow in March under glass for autumn picking. After the plants have been hardened off, set them out about 30cm/12in apart in rows 60cm/24in apart. Dip the roots in calomel paste before transplanting to help against clubroot. When the curds begin to form, fold the leaves over the hearts to keep them clean and white. Varieties: All the Year Round, Early Snowball, Veitch's Self-Protecting.

Celery

Self-blanching celery should be sown in boxes in early April and set out early in June about 20cm/8in apart. They must be kept well watered if they are not to be tough and stringy, and they will be ready for harvesting in September and October. Non-self-blanching celery must be planted in trenches and earthed up continually to prevent them becoming bitter. Frost will improve the flavour, so it is best to leave it until well into October. Varieties: Golden Self-Blanching, Lancashire Prize Red.

French Bean

These like a light warm soil, and should not be sown in the open until the risk of frost is past. Sow the seed at monthly intervals from the beginning of May until July for succession, in rows 30cm/12in apart. Seed should be sown 5cm/2in deep, and the plants spaced 20cm/8in apart. Give the plants plenty of water, and pick the beans young to encourage more to form. Varieties: The Prince, Earligreen.

Kohlrabi

This is a curious vegetable, a cross between a swede and a turnip, and is a member of the brassica family. Sow from April onwards in drills 40cm/15in apart, and thin the plants to 20cm/8in in the rows. Harvest the roots when they are not more than 10cm/4in across as they become woody after this. Varieties: Early Purple Vienna, Early White Vienna.

Leek

Leeks should really be grown in trenches with plenty of garden compost at the bottom, although they can be grown on the flat. Sow the seed in shallow drills in mid March, and set them out 15cm/6in apart in the trenches during June. This should be done by making a hole with a dibber, filling it with water and dropping the plant gently in. Earth the plants up as they grow to blanch the stems. They are very hardy and can be left in the ground right into spring; if frosts are expected, they will be difficult to dig

up, so lift them on a warmer day and lay them flat on the earth and they will come to no harm. Varieties: Clandon White, Marble Pillar.

Lettuce

Lettuce seed should be sown in a seedbed up till mid April, and the young plants set out 20cm/8in apart in the rows where they are to mature. After mid-April, transplanted lettuces will run to seed, so sow them in the rows and thin them out to the same distance. Keep them well watered. Varieties: Webb's Wonderful, Winter Density, Suzan, Tom Thumb, Buttercrunch.

Marrow/Courgette

These are in fact the same vegetable, the courgettes coming from plants which tend to produce smaller fruits. Sow the seeds in individual peat pots in April, setting the seeds on their edges about 1cm/½in below the soil level. Set them in a cold frame to harden off in May, and plant them out with plenty of manure or compost at the end of May or early in June. Allow 90–120cm/3–4ft between plants for the courgettes, and 150–180cm/5–6ft between the trailing varieties. Cut the fruits as soon as they reach a reasonable size to encourage more to form. Varieties: Butternut, Sutton's Superlative, Zucchini (courgette).

Above: no garden vegetable plot would be complete without lettuce
Left: leeks are easy to grow and generally disease-free

Protect cucumber fruits from contact with the soil

Mustard and Cress

Sowings should be made every two to three weeks almost throughout the year in small seedbeds. Cress is traditionally sown four days earlier than mustard so that both will mature together – this should take two to three weeks. Variety: Moss Curled.

Onion

Onions need a long growing season, and where this is not possible, in the north of England, Scotland and Ulster, it will be best to raise the crop from small onions called sets. If they are to be grown from seed, they should be sown in a heated greenhouse in January, set into boxes in March, and put into the open ground in April, 20cm/8in apart in rows 30cm/12in apart. If sets are used they should be planted also in April at the same distances.

Stop watering in August to encourage the bulbs to ripen, and assist this process still further by bending over the leaves just above the bulbs. The crop will be ready for harvesting in September; leave them on the soil for a few days to dry, and they can then be tied into ropes and stored in a cool dry place for autumn and winter use. Check stored onions regularly and throw out any which go bad as they may otherwise infect all the others. Varieties: Stuttgarter Giant, Ailsa Craig, Reliance.

Parsnip

Parsnips need very well dug soil as their roots can go down enormous lengths. They will never do well in stony ground, but if required, push 2·5cm/1in pipes into the soil to a depth of 30cm/12in and fill these with finely sifted soil. Sow a few seeds in each, and thin to one strong plant after germination. The roots will be ready to lift from early November, and will be greatly improved in flavour by a touch of frost. Canker is the worst parsnip complaint, and the best thing to do is to look out for varieties which have been specially bred to resist this. Varieties: Hollow Crown, Avonresister.

Pea

By planting early, mid season and late varieties, it is possible to have fresh peas from May until late September. In sheltered areas, round seeded

Peas almost ready for harvest

peas can be sown in November, otherwise successional sowings can be started in late January and continue until early June. Make a drill about 5cm/2in deep and 30cm/12in wide, and sow the peas in alternate rows of four and three across it, staggering the rows. Set pea sticks in the ground if you can get hold of them, otherwise fix a net for the tendrils to cling to so that the pods will be held off the ground.

The peas should be picked before the pods have become hard, as otherwise they will lose their sweetness and become starchy. Cut the pods rather than pull them from the plants, as the root system will not be very strong and you may otherwise pull the whole plant out. Varieties: Early Onward, Kelvedon Monarch, Kelvedon Wonder.

Potato
This is a staple part of everyone's diet, but can be hard work to cultivate. Buy Ministry of Agriculture certified seed potatoes, and set them in egg boxes or similar containers as soon as you get them with the sprouting ends upwards, in order to get good strong shoots before planting.

In sheltered parts, plant the early potatoes in March and the main crop in April; elsewhere, plant the main crop in early April and the more tender earlies at the end of the month.

Dig a trench to a depth of 20cm/8in, put 8cm/3in of compost in the bottom, then 8cm/3in of peat. Then press in the tuber with the sprouting end upmost, and cover them with soil. Stack the surplus soil on either side of the trench and use it to keep earthing up the plants

A fine crop of new potatoes

Radish

Radishes must be grown quickly, or they will become hard and woody and not be worth eating. This means they must be kept moist at all times. Sow the seeds thinly in shallow drills at three week intervals from early March for succession, and thin them to 5cm/2in in the rows. They can be grown between slow maturing crops, as they will be out of the way before sprouts or potatoes need the space between the rows. Last sowings should be made in July.

Club root can attack radishes, but normally they are grown and harvested before this disease has time to get a hold. Varieties: French Breakfast, Icicle, Inca, Cherry Belle.

Runner Bean

Runner beans represent tremendous value for the amount of space they take up, though the initial work in rowing them can be rather arduous. They are best grown against rows of sturdy stakes in the form of an inverted V anchored firmly at each end and with a long stake running the length of the row at the top.

Before sowing, dig a trench where the row is to be and fill it with compost as it is important that as much moisture as possible should be retained in the soil for the crop. The stakes should be 23cm/9in apart in each row with 30cm/12in width between them. Sow one seed 5cm/2in deep beside each stake, and a few extra at the end to replace any which fail to germinate. This should be done around mid-May in order to avoid any late frosts.

When the flowers have set, spray them with water at midday if possible, to encourage the beans to form. Pick them regularly once they begin to appear to ensure a supply from late July on. Varieties: Crusader, Streamline, Fry.

Shallot

Plant the sets in March, pressing them into the soil 25cm/10in apart, with 30cm/12in between the rows. Bend over the necks during August to encourage ripening, and harvest in September and allow the bulbs to dry. Variety: Dutch Yellow.

as they grow. Early potatoes should be 30cm/12in apart in the trenches, with 45cm/18in between the rows, and maincrop potatoes should be 45cm/18in apart in the trenches with 60cm/24in between rows.

Lift the plants when the foliage begins to die down, and store those which are not for immediate eating in a cool dry place. Potatoes suffer from a variety of diseases which can be controlled (see page 150), and very rarely from two which must be reported to the Ministry of Agriculture if they occur: Colorado beetle and wart disease. The beetle is black and orange striped; and wart disease appears as cauliflower shaped swellings on the tubers. Varieties: early; Arran Pilot, Home Guard, Foremost; maincrop: Pentland Crown, King Edward.

Rhubarb is easy to grow

Above: pick runner beans before
they get very long
Left: take the leaves off sprout
plants as the buttons begin to swell

Spinach

Seed should be sown in shallow drills 30cm/12in apart, and the plants should be thinned to 20cm/8in in the rows. They need planty of water, and tend to run to seed quickly in hot weather; they should be pulled up once this begins to happen. A much easier crop tasting very similar, is New Zealand spinach, which is not a member of the same family, but is grown in the same way. Varieties: Cleanleaf, Superb, Bloomsdale Longstanding.

Spring Onion

Seed should be sown in shallow drills in October, and again in early spring. Weeding between the plants is important if they are to reach a good size. Those from an autumn sowing will be ready in April, and spring sown ones in July. Varieties: White Lisbon, White Spanish.

Sprout

Seed should be sown in a seedbed in March, thinned early, and transplanted in April. Set the

A well-grown tomato truss

plants out 60cm/24in apart, with the same amount between the rows, and make the soil very firm around the base, or the sprouts will be loose and flavourless. Stake the plants in windy gardens. Sprouts taste better for a touch of frost, so do not start picking until after the first frost. Harvesting can continue until March of the following year. Varieties: Peer Gynt, Avoncross.

Swede

Seed is sown in early May, in drills 45cm/18in apart, and the seedlings thinned to 25cm/10in in the rows. They should be harvested when they are about tennis ball size for maximum sweetness; this will be around mid-October. They can be stored in a cool dry place. Variety: Purple Top Yellow.

Tomato

For greenhouse tomatoes, see page 105. For outdoor tomatoes, sow the seeds in a seed tray on a sunny windowsill in March, and prick them out into individual 8cm/3in pots as soon as they are large enough to handle. When the pots are filled with roots, pot them on into 13cm/5in pots.

Harden them off during late April and May, and plant them out in April; if you like, they can be grown in 25cm/10in pots outdoors on a patio.

If you do not get a lot of light in the house, you will be better advised to buy plants as seedlings raised with insufficient light will be thin, drawn and yellow. Tomatoes need good rich soil with plenty of potash, and a sunny site. Plant them firmly and stake them, tying the stems to the stake at 20cm/8in intervals. Pinch out the shoots which form between the main stem and the leaves branching off; otherwise there will be masses of marble sized fruits rather than a reasonable number of large tomatoes. After the plant has set five trusses of flowers, pinch out the growing tip as otherwise the fruit may not ripen before the autumn.

By the second week in September, pick all the tomatoes which are of full size but are still yellow or green and bring them indoors, either to put on a sunny windowsill until they ripen, or to be used in making chutney.

Pests and diseases are not as prevalent on outdoor tomatoes as on indoor grown ones; see page 154 for symptoms and cures. Varieties: Atom, Moneymaker, Ailsa Craig, Alicante, Sigmabush.

Turnip

For an early crop, sow in a frame at the end of February, as thinly as possible, and spacing the seedlings to 20cm/8in. They should be ready for eating by early May. Outdoors, sow early in April for July harvesting. They should be thinned to 15cm/6in, and will benefit if you dig in plenty of bonfire ash. They should be lifted by the very latest when they are tennis ball size, otherwise they will be hard and woody. Drills should be 30cm/12in apart, and sowings should be made every three to four weeks for succession. The crop can be stored in peat in a cool dry place. As members of the brassica family, they can suffer from club root, but like radishes, they are normally grown and harvested too quickly for the disease to get a hold. Varieties: Early Milan, Tokyo Cross, Golden Ball.

16 The Herb Garden

Some people prefer to collect plants in botanical groups, and herbs lend themselves rather well to this; for instance to take the family *Umbelliferae*, it contains a good many useful herbs such as lovage, fennel, coriander, and dill, and the *Labiatae* is another, with basil, balm, hyssop and marjoram counted among its members. Each family can have a bed devoted to it, and it is easy then, and rather surprising, to see how widely plants can differ within a family in habit, shape of leaf and even apparently in flower though a trained botanist will be able to pinpoint the similarities on which the classification is based. Collections of this kind can be seen at Kew, Cambridge and the Chelsea Physic Garden—the last mentioned is, however, only open for students and professional use.

Another way of collecting herbs is to grow only those which are pleasantly aromatic or perfumed; this would of course mean no parsley, no garlic, no savory and so on, but it does leave room for quite a lot more plants, such as lavender, thyme, lemon balm, basil and mint. Some need bruising before releasing their fragrance, and growing them on paths or at the edges of beds close to paths, will ensure the necessary pressure.

One of the nicest and most satisfying ways to grow herbs is to collect them together into a small garden within a garden. It is much easier, then, to give them the special attention and conditions that they like. Most of them prefer sun and shelter from wind, and the kind of soil vegetables do best in. Paving seems to lend itself to herbs, as it gives definition to their sometimes rather untidy growth, and it can be used in a kind of chess board pattern or laid out like the spokes of a wheel. The carpeting herbs can take the place of paving such as creeping thyme or chamomile, if paving is unobtainable.

Hedges round the herb garden will help to shelter it, and climbers trained up trellis work or similar supports; the hedges can be of herbs themselves such as lavender, rosemary, sage, or *Rosa gallica officinalis*–the Apothecaries' rose. If the garden is to be laid out in a square it could have a bed in each corner, with a centre such as a pool, sundial, or bird bath. A seat in the centre or to one side will always be popular, so that the fragrance and aroma of the herbs can be enjoyed; there is a certain old world peacefulness about a herb garden, too, which is best absorbed by lingering. If you have cats, they will nearly always be found in it somewhere peacefully asleep, knowing that they are least likely to be disturbed there. Beware, however if you plant nepeta (catmint)–the peace will not be quite so absolute, as cats tear it to pieces in their attempts to become one with it.

However you decide to lay out your herb garden, try to design it on paper beforehand. Then you can be sure of blending the colours of foliage and flowers, and avoid the mistake of planting tall herbs in front of the mound-forming kinds. Some herbs have beautifully coloured leaves; others have an architectural habit of growth with handsomely shaped leaves; some die down completely in winter, others have attractive flowers and all this should be taken into account when designing a herb garden. One needs to know, too, the amount of space a plant will take up in girth as well as height.

The smallest outdoor area will have room for a herb collection

Herbs – a Descriptive List

Angelica *(Angelica archangelica; Umbelliferae)*
Description A tall, stout plant 2–3 × 1m/ 5–8 × 3ft, perennial if prevented from flowering, otherwise biennial. Large, dark green leaves divided into leaflets, and flat, spreading heads of creamy white flowers in July. Origin Northern Hemisphere, introduced 1568.

Uses Young green stems and leaf stalks used for candying for cakes and dessert decoration, picked April-May. Leaves also sometimes used in cooking. Plant strongly flavoured in all its parts, reminiscent of juniper berries, said to be used in making the French liqueur Chartreuse. Roots recommended for medicinal use as a digestive and for blood cleansing.

Cultivation Put in small plants in spring and divide roots when established; seeds will distribute themselves in due course. If using seed, sow as soon as ripe in August, as viability is lost very quickly, thin out when large enough to handle, or plant in permanent positions in autumn, about 45cm/18in apart. Moist soil and semi-shady place preferred.

Balm, lemon *(Melissa officinalis; Labiatae)*
Description A hardy herbaceous perennial 60–100 × 45cm/2–3 × 1½ft, rather shrub-like in form. Leaves are soft, heart-shaped and wrinkled; whitish flowers are produced June-August. Origin, Europe, naturalized in Britain; used since the Middle Ages. Top growth dies to ground in winter, but new shoots appear very early in spring.

Uses The strongly lemon scented leaves are used in drinks, also in salads, sauces and omelettes. It is said to be useful for indigestion and to relieve tension. A favourite plant for pot pourri and perfumery, and is a plant liked by bees because the flowers contain much nectar.

Cultivation Easily grown by division of established plants in autumn, or from seeds sown in spring in a frame. Germination takes 3–4 weeks, and young plants are put out early in September. Will grow in most soils and situations, but does best in sun and moist, well drained soil. Remove flowers to encourage leaf production.

Basil, sweet *(Ocimum basilicum, Labiatae)*
Description Half hardy annual 60–90 ×

30cm/2–3 × 1ft; light green, soft hairy leaves up to 7cm/3in long; white flowers in August. Dwarf basil, a variety of this, grows to 15–22cm/6–9in. Origin, tropical Asia, Africa and the Pacific Islands; introduced in 1548.

Uses Leaves strongly and sweetly aromatic, similar to clove, used in cookery, particularly in Italy, and in India for curries. Because of its powerful flavour, sparing use should be made of it. The oil is used in perfume, and medicinally it is particularly of help in curing headaches and migraines.

Cultivation Sow seed in 13–16°C/55–60°F in March; germination will take about a fortnight. Prick out, harden off and plant indoors in late May 20cm/9in apart, in sandy rich soil and a sunny position. Seedlings transplant badly, so either sow generously inside or sow outdoors in mid May, and thin later. Water freely in dry weather; pinch out the tops for bushiness. Dwarf basil is best for pot cultivation. Lift in early September and pot up, for early winter use, cutting back the top growth hard

Bay, sweet *(Laurus nobilis; Lauraceae)*

Description A large, evergreen shrub or tree, not hardy in severe cold; can form a tree 6m/20ft tall in southern England. Insignificant pale yellow flowers in May, followed by black berries in hot summers. Origin, southern Europe, possibly introduced 1548.

Uses Leaves strongly flavoured and much used in cooking, stews, or as part of a bouquet garni. Berries and leaves much used formerly for medicinal purposes.

Cultivation Any soil and a sunny, sheltered place suit it. Young plants are put in during autumn or spring; heel cuttings can be taken in April, or 7–10cm/3–4in half-ripe cuttings in August in a cold frame, in pots, potting-on as required. Plant out next autumn in nursery bed for two years. Clip trained plants twice in July and September. A good container plant as pyramid or standard.

Bergamot *(Monarda didyma; Labiatae)*

Description A hardy perennial often grown in the herbaceous border, which dies down to the crown each autumn. Height 30–60cm/1–2ft, spread 30cm/1ft. Heads of tubular bright red flowers appear June-August. Origin, eastern America, introduced 1656. Also known as Oswego Tea, or Bee Balm.

Uses The orange-scented leaves are mainly used for making tea, and on the Continent as a sleep-inducing tisane. They are also added to other drinks, chopped up for salads and occasionally used in pot pourri.

Cultivation Monarda prefers damp soil and does well at the waterside in sunny, open or semi-shady places. Plant in autumn or spring, mulch with compost each year at these times also. Cut back in autumn to tidy. Increase by dividing in spring.

Borage *(Borago officinalis; Boraginacea)*

Description A hardy annual to 90cm/3ft tall and 45cm/1½ft wide, with large leaves to 22cm/9in long, rough and hairy, and brilliant blue flowers in drooping clusters from June to September. Origin uncertain – it may be a native plant, or it may be naturalised as a garden escape. It has been widely grown here in Britain, however, at least since Elizabethan times.

Uses The cucumber-like flavour that the fresh leaves and flowers give to drinks or salads is very refreshing; the flowers are used to give colour to pot pourri, or candied for cake decoration. It was once used medicinally for inflammations and redness of the eyes.

Cultivation Sow seed outdoors in September or April, thinning to 30cm/12in apart in ordinary soil. Flowering will be in May, or June-July, depending on time of sowing. For winter cultivation indoors, sow seeds in containers in September. Flowering may continue through a mild winter.

Caraway *(Carum carvi; Umbelliferae)*

Description A taprooted, hardy biennial to 60cm/2ft tall, with frond-like, much divided leaves, and umbels of small white flowers in the second June after sowing seed. Origin, Europe to India, cultivated in Britain for many centuries, possibly since the time of the Romans.

Uses The small, black, narrow seeds are the

seed of the seedcake, or caraway cake; they are also used in biscuits, bread and cheese, in fact in very many dishes and recipes. Young roots can be used as a vegetable rather like parsnip or carrot, and the leaves in salads. Oil from the seeds is used to perfume brown Windsor soap, and some Continental liqueurs, for instance Kummel.

Cultivation Seeds are sown outdoors in spring in rows 30cm/12in apart, thinning to the same distance. Supply a well drained soil and sunny place–winter waterlogging will kill it. Harvest the seeds in July-August the following year.

Chamomile (Anthemis nobilis; Compositae)

Description Roman chamomile is a low growing herbaceous perennial 15–22cm/6–9in tall, spreading to about 30cm/12in. Leaves very finely cut and fern-like forming a thick covering; white daisy flowers about 2½cm/1in wide from June-August. There is a non-flowering strain called the Treneague strain. It remains green through the winter. Origin: a native plant. There is also *Matricaria chamomilla,* wild chamomile, also a native plant, very similar in appearance, but taller, to about 40cm/15in; this is an annual.

Uses Roman chamomile is used mainly for small lawns; it has some medicinal properties. Wild chamomile flowers are used considerably in medicine, and for shampoos. A tisane made of the flowers which helps in digestion is popular on the Continent, and a concentrated infusion acts as an emetic. All parts of the plant are strongly aromatic.

Cultivation Roman chamomile can be grown from rooted cuttings put out in spring in a sandy soil and sunny place about 15cm/6in apart for a lawn, or about 30cm/12in apart, if grown as a herb. Chamomile lawns are cut three or four times a year. Seed is sown in spring outdoors and later thinned, or is sown indoors under glass in February.

Chervil (Anthriscus cerefolium; Umbelliferae)

Description A hardy biennial usually grown as an annual with delicate much cut and lacy leaves, flowering stems to 45cm/18in and small white flowers in clusters from June to August in the second year from sowing. Origin, south-eastern Europe naturalized in some places.

Uses Leaves have slightly peppery and parsley-like flavour and are the part used, mainly for cooking, in sauces, soup and salads and in particular in omelette fines herbes. Chervil has a medicinal value in cleansing the blood and clearing skin troubles.

Cultivation Sow seed outdoors in succession at four-week intervals from February to October in a well drained soil, in drills, thinning to 30cm/12in apart. It does not like drying out. Cut the leaves about 6–8 weeks after sowing, and a further crop will be produced. An August sowing will give leaves in September–October and early spring, or earlier if protected by cloches. Window boxes and pots are also suitable for overwintering. The seed loses its viability quickly.

Chives (Allium schoenoprasum; Alliaceae)

Description Perennial bulbous plants with tubular, grasslike leaves to 10–25cm/4–10in, which die down to ground level in late autumn. Round heads of purple flowers in June-July. There is a giant variety, to 45cm/18in tall, much less well-flavoured. Origin, the Northern Hermisphere but rarely found naturally in Britain.

Uses Almost exclusively in cooking, for the delicate onion flavour of the leaves. Seldom used medicinally, though they are said to have some slight good effect on digestion.

Cultivation Sow seeds outdoors in spring 25cm/10in apart in drills in medium to heavy soil and sun or shade; thin to clumps about 15cm/16in apart. Also increase by dividing in spring or autumn. Remove the flowers to encourage leaf production; water well in dry weather. Mulch in autumn with garden compost. Cover with cloches to protect from frost as long as possible, or pot up and grow in an indoor window sill in 15cm/6in pots.

Coriander (Coriandrum sativum; Umbelliferae)

Description A hardy annual 45 × 20cm/ 18 × 8in with delicate deeply cut, stem leaves;

Chives have pretty flowers as well
as an excellent flavour

the base leaves are more solidly lobed. Both types have a very unpleasant strong smell. Tiny white flowers, tinted violet, are produced in flat heads in June-July. The round seeds are ripe in August. Origin: southern Europe, naturalized in Britain.

Uses The seeds are the part which is used most; they have a strong and unpleasant odour when unripe, but the disappearance of this indicates their ripeness; in fact their fragrance improves with age. The flavour is a mixture of lemon and sage. Powder of the seeds is much used in cooking, for instance curry, drinks including liqueurs and in both meat and desert dishes of Spain, Greece, the Middle East and India.

Cultivation Sow the seeds out of doors in April, preferably in a warm soil, otherwise germination is slow, in rows about 30cm/12in apart, thinning to 15cm/6in. Also in September,

or under glass in March, to plant out in May. Collect the seeds in August when their unpleasant smell has gone.

Dill *(Anethum graveolens; Umbelliferae)*
Description A hardy annual 60–90 × 30cm/2–3 × 1ft, rather like fennel to look at, with ferny, very finely divided leaves, and a stout stem; small dull yellow flowers come in large clusters between June and August. Origin, the Mediterranean countries; has been grown in Britain since the Roman occupation.

Uses Mostly culinary, in the case of the leaves, for salads, fish and vegetables; the seeds have a bitter taste but supply gripe water and are otherwise useful for digestion. The seeds are also mildly sleep inducing.

Cultivation Sow seeds outdoors in March-April in a moist but draining soil, in sun. Germination takes 14–21 days depending on the

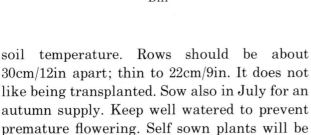

Dill

Right:
a fennel plant

rootstock. A native of southern Europe, naturalized in Britain for many centuries, particularly near southern coasts and estuaries.

Uses The leaves have a strong and unusual flavour, and are used in cooking, mostly with fish. The basal stems of Florence fennel are eaten as a vegetable. Medicinally it was thought to have weight reducing properties; the liquid is used to make a solution for bathing the eyes. It can also be used as part of a face pack.

Cultivation Sow seed outdoors in April in sun or slight shade and a moist, chalky soil, in rows 45cm/1½ft apart, thinning to 45–60cm/1½–2ft and stake the plant as it grows. Finnoccio needs a good warm summer, plenty of moisture and a rich soil; the base of the stem should be earthed up as it begins to swell so as to blanch it. For winter use, transplant into pots and keep indoors or under glass.

Garlic (*Allium sativum; Alliaceae*)

Description A hardy perennial usually grown as an annual in Britain, with a bulbous base made of separate segments called cloves, and grass-like leaves about 30cm/12in tall. Flower stem to 60cm/24in, and flower white, appearing in summer. Origin doubtful, possibly the Kirghiz desert of Central Asia, but now grows naturally throughout the world including Britain.

Uses Has very strong flavour and odour, mostly onion-like, but with a characteristic all its own; this makes it a herb to use sparingly in cooking, where it has widespread use. Thought to have considerable antiseptic and antibiotic

soil temperature. Rows should be about 30cm/12in apart; thin to 22cm/9in. It does not like being transplanted. Sow also in July for an autumn supply. Keep well watered to prevent premature flowering. Self sown plants will be stronger than their parents.

Fennel (*Foeniculum vulgare; Umbelliferae*)

Description A tall, stout hardy perennial 150–200cm/5–8ft tall by about 60cm/24in with a long white carrot-like root, rather short lived. Very finely cut, fern-like leaves, branching stems, and flat-headed clusters of yellow flowers in late summer. The variety *dulce* or *azoricum* is Florence fennel or finnochio, with a bulbous

qualities particularly for stomach infections and blood cleansing.

Cultivation Plant the cloves in mid February, March or between September and early November, in a light rich soil and sunny place. Distance apart about 20cm/8in, just below the soil surface, in rows 30cm/12in apart. Remove the flowering stems. Harvest when the leaves are yellow and hang to dry in a warm but shady place. Use a new site every year to avoid attack by white rot.

Horseradish *(Armoracia rusticana; Cruciferae)*
Description A stout perennial to 60cm/24in tall, with large basal leaves 30–60cm/12–24in long and small white flowers in May. The roots are fleshy and fanged. Origin, eastern Europe, naturalised in Britain, and sometimes a pernicious weed.
Uses Now mainly used in cooking, the peppery roots being grated, and used for horseradish sauce in particular. Also antibiotic qualities and much good effect on digestion. Was formerly prescribed against scurvy.
Cultivation Supply a rich, moist soil worked to 60cm/24in depth. Plant 8cm/3in root cuttings in March 30cm/12in apart, just covered with soil, in a bed separate from other plants. Lift all the plants in late autumn, store the larger roots in sand for cooking, and retain the smaller, also in sand, for planting next spring. Regular new plantings thus ensure the best quality roots for cooking.

Hyssop *(Hyssopus officinalis; Labiatae)*
Description A shrub-like, hardy perennial, semi-evergreen, to 45cm/18in × 30cm/12in wide. Pink, white or blue-violet flowers in July. Leaves narrow, like rosemary, but much less leathery. Origin, Mediterranean area and east to Central Asia.
Uses The aromatic leaves have a mint-like odour, and are slightly bitter and peppery, so use in cooking should be sparing. Hyssop is used in Chartreuse liqueur. Medicinally hyssop tea has some use for catarrh and for clearing up bruises, and a further use is in perfume, especially eau-de-cologne.

Cultivation Sow seed in April outdoors, thinning to 30cm/12in apart in rows 45cm/18in apart. Take 5cm/2in cuttings in April-May in peat/sand, and put in a cold frame. Pot up when rooted and plant out in autumn. Bought-in plants are planted in autumn or spring. A heavy, wet soil and a cold winter are likely to kill it.

Lemon-scented verbena *(Lippia citriodora; Verbenaceae)*
Description A tender, shrubby plant, to 120cm/4ft, although 3–5m/10–15ft in its native Chile. Hardy in the West country outdoors. Shining, long-pointed, narrow leaves with lilac flowers in fluffy clusters in August. Introduced 1784.
Uses Strongly lemon flavoured leaves used in cooking and for tea, much drunk in Spain. Helps to ease troubles in the respiratory tract, as well as being pleasantly flavoured. Also added to pot-pourri.
Cultivation Grow from tip cuttings taken in spring, rooted under glass in warmth. Pot on as required and, after hardening off, plant out in late May–June in a sunny sheltered place, and dryish, rather poor soil. Mulch heavily for winter or lift and pot up in autumn for indoor growth, cutting it back by about half.

Lovage *(Levisticum officinale; Umbelliferae)*
Description A perennial with stout, hollow stems to 2m/6ft tall; it has fleshy roots and toothed leaves divided into leaflets like celeriac. Tiny, greenish yellow flowers appear in clusters in July. Origin, the Mediterranean area. May have been introduced by the Romans.
Uses Strong celery aroma and flavour from entire plant the whole of which (except the roots) is used in cooking, especially for soups and casseroles, giving a yeast-like flavour. Medicinal uses included relief of eye troubles, as a gargle and mouthwash, and as a deodorant, using the leaves in bath water.
Cultivation Sow the seeds when ripe in late August-September as the period of viability is short, and transplant the following spring to 1m/3ft apart, in moist well drained soil. Mulch every year. Also increase from root cuttings,

each with an eye, in spring, put 5cm/2in below soil level.

Marjoram, sweet or knotted (Origanum majorana; Labiatae)

Description A half-hardy annual 20cm/18in tall, rather bushy, with small greyish green slightly hairy leaves, and round green 'knots' from which tiny pinkish flowers come from June onwards. Origin, North Africa, introduced 1573. *O. vulgare* is a native plant of chalk downland, commonly called Oregano.

Uses Sweet and unusual aroma to the leaves, which are much used, both fresh and dried in cooking; especially good for flavouring sausages. Also used in perfumery and has mild antiseptic qualities, due to the thymol content.

Cultivation Sow seed outdoors in rows 30cm/12in apart, in mid May, earlier in warm sheltered gardens, and thin to 25cm/10in apart. Provide a sunny place, and fertile, medium soil. Seedlings are slow to grow; weeding is important. Good for pot cultivation, but pot marjoram (*O. onites*) will be needed for winter use. This is perennial, but less well flavoured. Trim hard back in late summer and pot up in autumn.

Marjoram

Mint (Mentha species; Labiatae)

Description Perennial, mostly hardy herbaceous plants, with wide-spreading roots, stems to 30–60cm/12–24in, and rounded or pointed leaves. Inconspicuous purplish or white flowers in July-August. Species cultivated: *M. spicata*, common mint, spearmint; *M. rotundifolia*, apple mint, smelling of apples; *M. citrata* 'Eau de Cologne'; *M. rotundifolia variegata*, green and cream edged leaves; pineapple mint, will not survive winter cold and damp. *M. piperita*, pepper mint.; *M. aquatica*, water mint. Origin, Europe including Britain.

Uses Mainly culinary, the leaves having varying fragrances and flavours as above. Leaves contain menthol and are good for summer drinks, and *M. citrata* is said to be an ingredient of Chartreuse liqueur. *M. piperita* leaves make a good digestive tea, so also does *M. aquatica*. Pepper mint is much used also in confectionery.

Cultivation Plant between autumn and spring; propagate by division at these seasons also, or lift rooted stems and plant these. Damp soil is preferred, but it grows so easily that it needs curbing rather than encouraging, except for pineapple mint, which is slow to grow and less vigorous. It is advisable to root cuttings of this and keep them in the greenhouse through the winter; all will grow well in containers. If rust infects the plants, (small red-brown spots on leaves and stems) destroy them and plant afresh in a different place.

Nettles (Urtica species; Urticaceae)

Description Hardy perennial and annual plants, which reach 30–145cm/1–5ft, having pointed toothed leaves and green flowers in summer. *U. urens* is annual, 30cm/12in and flowers all season; *U. dioica* is perennial; both are native, but *U. pilulifera* was introduced by the Romans and has flowers in rounded clusters. It is annual and grows to 60cm/24in.

Uses Leaves picked young are a substitute for spinach; they contain iron and silicic acid, and are good for cleaning the blood in spring. They are a good diuretic. The fibres were once used to make into a kind of linen, before cotton came into widespread use. The stinging feeling produced by the leaves is due to a substance similar to histamin and similar to the hormone secreted by the pancreas.

Cultivation   As it is such a well known weed, advice on this seems unnecessary.

Parsley *(Petroselinum crispum; Umbelliferae)*
Description   A hardy biennial usually grown as an annual, to about 30cm/12in by 15cm/6in wide; it is thinly taprooted with very much cut and curled leaves, and tiny green-yellow flowers in flat-headed clusters from June to August. Origin, central and southern Europe; naturalized in Britain.

Uses   Leaves strong and distinctive flavour, widely used in cooking. It contains an appreciable quantity of vitamin C, so has a useful nutritional quality, and stimulates the digestion. Parsley water is said to be good for encouraging the disappearance of freckles.

Cultivation   Sow in March-April for a summer crop in moist fertile soil and sun or shade; rows should be 30cm/12in apart, with 15cm/16in in the row. A warm soil will speed germination, which can take 10–28 days. For winter use, sow in July, and protect in winter with cloches if snow is likely. Remove flowerheads to encourage leaves. It is a good container herb; for pots a 12cm/5in size is best.

Rosemary *(Rosmarinus officinalis; Labiatae)*
Description   An evergreen shrub, hardy except in severe weather and wet soils, to about 120cm/4ft in gardens by about 145cm/5ft. Very narrow, dark green leaves $2\frac{1}{2}$cm/1in long, and pale purple flowers in May. Originally southern Europe and Asia Minor, probably introduced in the Middle Ages.

Uses   The leaves are pungently and pleasantly aromatic, giving a distinctive flavour in cooking; the oil contained in them is similar to eucalyptus. Rosemary is said to have an invigorating effect, and helps in restoring energy. It can also be used to improve the condition of skin and hair.

Cultivation   Plant in a sunny place and well-drained soil in spring; regular use will do all the

Rosemary

pruning necessary. Easily increased from tip cuttings taken in March, putting four in a 10cm/4in pot in a frame or greenhouse. Later cuttings in August are also possible.

Sage *(Salvia officinalis; Labiatae)*
Description   An evergreen shrub, hardy except in severe winters and damp soil. Height: 60cm/24in with the same spread. Grey-green, wrinkled, slightly woolly leaves, with purple of white flowers in early summer. Origin, southern Europe and the Mediterranean area, introduced in 1597 or earlier.

Uses   The strongly aromatic, slightly bitter leaves are much used in cooking, in particular with pork or duck. Sage tea is said to be good for gargling and as a mouth wash; it helps in the digestion, and in clearing a stuffy head if the steam from an infusion is inhaled.

Cultivation   Plant is spring in well-drained soil and a sunny place, in moderate fertility. A heavy wet soil is to be avoided. Easily grown from seed sown in late April, which takes about three weeks to germinate; also increased from 8cm/3in cuttings taken in August and put in a cold frame. Pot on singly and plant out the following spring.

Salad burnet *(Sanguisorba minor; Rosaceae)*
Description   A decorative, hardy, herbaceous perennial, low growing, with flower stems to 30–45cm/12–18in toothed leaves are pinnate and nearly evergreen, and purple tinted round heads of tiny green flowers come all summer. Origin, Europe; native to this country.

Uses   Mainly for the leaves which are cucumber flavoured and put in salads, soups and drinks. Used in the same ways as borage. Also said to have value as a tonic.

Cultivation   Easily grown, salad burnet prefers light soil. Sow seed when ripe in summer, or the following spring, thinning plants to 23cm/9in apart. Established plants can be increased by division in early spring. It makes a good container herb.

Savory *(Satureia* species; *Labiatae)*
Description   *Satureia hortensis,* summer savory; an annual plant to 20cm/8in with narrow leaves 1cm/$\frac{1}{2}$in long, and pale lilac flowers in spikes from July-September. *S. montana,* winter savory; a hardy perennial, semi-evergreen, subshrub to 35cm/15in, otherwise similar to summer savory. Origin, southern Europe, introduced around 1562, or earlier.

Uses   Leaves are strongly aromatic, nearer to a spice than a herb, used in cooking, mainly to flavour beans, but also in salads, soups and with fish; gather the leaves before the flowers appear. The savories are good bee plants. The leaves are sometimes used to help in digestion.

Cultivation   Summer savory is grown from seed sown in April in rows 30cm/12in apart, thinned to 15cm/6in. The leaves can be gathered twice, in August and in October, for drying. Cover the seed lightly, otherwise germination is poor. Winter savory can also be grown from seed, by division in spring, or from 5cm/2in cuttings taken in May, put in a frame, and then potted on and planted out the following spring.

Sorrel, French or buckler-leaved *(Rumex scutatus; Polygonaceae)*
Description   A hardy perennial, rather sprawling plant, dying down every autumn; height of flowering stems to 30cm/12in, with a similar spread. Leaves are rounded shielded shaped, about 4cm/1$\frac{1}{2}$in wide, slightly fleshy; insignificant greenish flowers appear in summer. Origin, Europe, North Africa, West Asia; introduced but sometimes naturalized in this country.

Uses   The rather bitter leaves are very good for soup, but otherwise should be used sparingly for flavouring as they are very strong tasting. Also said to have diuretic qualities and to contain vitamin C.

Cultivation   Plant in spring or early autumn in moist, slightly heavy soil allowing 30cm/12in between the plants; remove the flowering stems to encourage leaf production. Divide in spring or sow seed in April, thinning when large enough to handle.

Tansy *(Chrysanthemum* or *Tanacetum vulgare; Compositae)*
Description   A hardy herbaceous perennial to 60cm/24in, with toothed leaves cut almost pinnately, up to 12cm/5in long, and small, flat, heads of yellow flowers from July-September. Origin, Europe, native to this country. There is a curled leaved form.

Uses   The leaves are strongly aromatic, rather like camphor, and can be used in the same way that mint is with roast lamb; they have many other culinary uses. Tansy tea was used for colds and rheumatism, and a distillation of the leaves is said to be good for the complexion, removing freckles and sunburn.

Cultivation   Easily grown, as would be expected of a native plant; any soil and situation will suit it. Division of the plant in spring is the usual method of increase, putting each piece 30cm/12in apart. It needs controlling, otherwise spread is rapid.

Tarragon *(Artemisia dracunculus: Compositae)*
Description   An evergreen perennial, hardy unless the weather is very cold or the soil badly drained, particularly winter; to 60cm/2ft tall, spreading to 60cm/24in. Leaves narrow and linear, with insignificant greyish flowers. The French variety is the best because of its flavour. Origin, southern Europe, introduced 1548.

Uses The leaves have an unusual and particularly pleasant flavour, and are used to make tarragon vinegar and for all sorts of savoury dishes. Also for sauce tartare and mustard.

Cultivation A well-drained, even dryish soil is essential, and preferably a sunny sheltered place, though an exposed site will do, if the soil is light. Plant in spring or September at 60cm/24in apart, and transplant about four years after the original planting, to maintain the flavour. Increase by division in spring. Seed does not set in this country. Protect in severe weather. Container cultivation is not easy, but the skilled gardener may like to pot up a few plants.

Thyme *(Thymus vulgaris; Labiatae)*

Description Common thyme is a hardy evergreen shrublet to 20cm/8in tall, spreading to 30cm/12in and more; tiny leaves, and lilac coloured flowers from June-August.

T. × citriodorus is similar but with broader, lemon-scented leaves. Origin, southern Europe, introduced before 1548.

Uses Considerable culinary uses for the highly aromatic leaves, particularly with meat and savoury dishes generally, and in Benedictine liqueur, also lemon thyme in custard. The essential oil, thymol, is the part which helps coughs, and catarrh. Thyme is said to have considerable germicidal action. Also good for baths, and is used in toothpaste. Lemon thyme is used in perfumery.

Cultivation Easily grown by dividing in spring, or from 2cm/1in long cuttings taken in early summer, put in a frame, potted on when rooted, and planted out in September. Seed is sown in spring (not lemon thyme) and treated in the same way, the final distance between plants being 30cm/12in either way. A sunny place and a light soil are preferred, preferably alkaline. It is a good container plant.

17 Fruit

Fresh fruit from the garden is always tastier than that bought in shops, and with the price of fruit going up all the time, it makes sense to grow some of your own. However small your garden there is nearly always room for a few plants—how about strawberry plants in a tub on the patio?

If you do have a small garden however, grow bushy varieties rather than tall ones—some apple and pear trees will crop heavily when grown in large pots. Do you have an unoccupied sunny wall? If so, you could grow peaches or apricots against it, although this may not be advisable in the north of England or Scotland—try an apple tree instead.

Soil

Most fruits are not too fussy about soil, and will do well in most kinds, as long as plenty of humus has been dug in. The plants and trees will need a deeply worked soil, as most of them send down their roots to a considerable depth. Digging should be carried out in the autumn, and the clods of earth left and not broken up; the frost will do this. If your soil is heavy, dig in peat, and add some lime to all kinds of soil unless yours is already exceptionally alkaline.

Apples

Apples are probably the most popular fruit amongst British gardeners. They grow best in a rich, well-drained soil. Trees can be planted whenever the soil is in good conditions between November and March. There should be about 15cm/6in of soil over the lower roots. Make sure the hole is large enough for the roots to be well spread out.

Types of Tree

Bush trees are pruned so that their centres are open; the main lateral should be cut back to 50cm/20in, and other laterals will grow out sideways from below this point to form the branches. After two years the tips should be taken off these branches, and new laterals which come out should be cut back to half their length each winter. Spur forming apples can be planted as cordons alongside paths. They are trained against wires and planted at an angle to restrict growth.

A compact, heavy cropping tree will be built up quickly from a dwarf pyramid. The leader is cut out when the tree is about 1m/3ft high, and at the end of each summer, all sideshoots are cut back to half the new season's wood. A standard tree is one allowed to grow to 2m/6ft tall; then the leader shoot is cut out and the tree built up in the same way as a bush tree.

Pests and Diseases

Aphis attacks all fruits, laying eggs in the winter and hatching in the spring to feed on the young shoots. Spray with tar oil in January for control. *Apple suckers* turn the flower buds brown; spraying with tar oil early in the year gives control. *Blossom weevils* eat into the flower buds; spray with tar oil in January. *Codling moth* makes apples maggoty; it can be prevented by spraying with derris in July. *Woolly aphis* can cause the branches to crack: spray with tar oil in January.

Apple trees are available in many different sizes

Brown rot causes the fruit to turn brown in store; burn diseased fruit and spray the trees with lime sulphur in March.

Varieties

For chalk soils: 'Charles Ross', 'Barnack Orange'. For clay soils: 'Newton Wonder', 'James Grieve', 'Adam's Pearmain'. On wet land: 'Laxton's Superb', 'Grenadier'. For sandy soil: 'Cox's Orange Pippin', 'Worcester Pearmain', 'Ellison's Orange'.

Pollinators

Most varieties need trees of another sort to pollinate them and ensure good crops. Normally, those varieties which bloom at the same time will pollinate one another. Some apples, such as 'Bramley's Seedling' are sterile and cannot pollinate other varieties; they must be planted with two other sorts to ensure fruit on all. The following groups are compatible amongst themselves.

1) 'Beauty of Bath', 'Laxton's Fortune', 'Lord Lambourne', 'Miller's Seedling'.
2) 'Bramley's Seedling', 'Cox's Orange Pippin', 'Egremont Russet', 'Ellison's Orange', 'Grenadier', 'James Grieve', 'Worcester Pearmain'.
3) 'Blenheim Orange', 'Charles Ross', 'Laxton's Superb', 'Sunset'.
4) 'Crawley Beauty', 'Edward VII', 'Royal Jubilee'.

Pears

Pears are grown in very similar fashion to apples, but it is in general the case that they need great warmth and shelter. They also need

Pears need a protected site as they flower early

more humus, and it is very important that the roots should not be allowed to dry out. It is important to bear pollination in mind when selecting varieties: the following groups are compatible amongst themselves.
1) 'Beurre Superfin', 'Conference', 'Louise Bonne'.
2) 'Clapp's Favourite', 'Josephine de Malines', 'William's Bon Chrétien'.
3) 'Doyenné du Comice', 'Dr Jules Guyot', 'Laxton's Superb'.

Pests and Diseases
Blossom weevil and *Codling moth;* see under Apples for means of control. *Leaf blister midge* causes reddish brown blisters on the leaves and fruit; spray with lime sulphur in April (not on 'Doyenné du Comice'). *Pear midge* maggots burrow into the fruit; dust or spray the trees with derris in March to give control. *Tortrix moth* and *Winter moth* feed on the blossom and leaves; control of the first can be gained by spraying with Abol-X in May, June and July, and the second with tar oil sprays in January. *Canker* appears as red bodies surrounding a branch; the whole branch should be cut out at the stem, and the wound treated with a proprietary sealing product. *Scab* causes black blisters on the shoots and fruits; control by spraying with Bordeau mixture at bud burst.

Plums

Plums can be grown as bush, standard or half standard trees, or as fans against south or west facing walls. They do best in a warm dry summer following a cold winter. They prefer high ground if the site is not too exposed, and if you live in a frost area, plant later flowering varieties such as 'Oullin's Golden Gage' and 'Belle de Louvin'.

Soil
Plums like a heavy loam, and do especially well above a chalky subsoil. Add lime before planting if your soil tends to be acid. To plant a tree against a wall, dig a hole 45cm/18in deep, put some mortar (for lime) at the bottom. Spread out

Plums ready for picking

the roots, and cover them with soil mixed with manure or bonemeal. The stem should be 15cm/6in from the wall. The trees will grow to a height of about 3m/10ft.

Very little pruning is needed, and if it is done, this should be in March. Early in summer, pinch back the sideshoots to encourage fruiting spurs to form.

Pollination
Some plums are self-fertile and will set fruit with their own pollen; others are partly so; and some are self-sterile and must have a pollinator. Plums flower only for three weeks, but this is not a serious problem as most varieties flower at the same time.

Pests and Diseases
Red spider is especially troublesome on trees growing against walls—the red insects suck the sap from below the leaves. Spray with DNOC while the trees are dormant. *Sawfly* attacks the pollen while the trees are in bloom, and should be prevented by spraying with Lindex in spring. *Brown rot:* see under Apples. *Canker:* see under Pears. *Silver leaf* is the most serious plum disease, the foliage turning silver, and the tree

Cherries are not easy to grow, but worth a try

dying soon after. 'Czar' and 'Victoria' are the most susceptible varieties. Pruning has to be finished (by law) before 15 July, to allow the wounds time to heal to reduce the risk of infection; broken branches should be treated with white lead paint.

Varieties
Late July to early August: 'Black Prince', 'Czar', 'Deniston's Superb'. Mid to end August: 'Oullin's Golden Gage', 'Victoria'. September: 'Bryanston Gage', 'Count Althann's Gage', 'Laxton's Delicious'. Early October: 'Merryweather' (a damson).

Cherries

Cherries are the most difficult fruit to grow in the garden. They do best as standards or half standards or fan trained trees against a wall, but can take up to ten years to produce crops of any size. As standards, they grow too tall for the average garden. None are self pollinating, and only limited numbers of varieties will pollinate each other.

Birds are a difficult problem; as the trees grow to a fair size, netting is not really a viable proposition, and you must be prepared to lose some of your crop to the birds. Cherries also bloom early and may be damaged by frost. Having said all this, it must be remembered that there is nothing nicer than a plate of juicy ripe cherries on a July afternoon.

Soil
Cherries need a dry sunny climate, and do not often do well north of the Trent. Work in some lime before planting in November, and allow 6m/20ft between standard trees. Pruning is carried out in spring, and it is important not to damage the bark, or bacterial canker or silver leaf may enter the wound and kill the tree.

Where cherries are grown against a wall, they will reach a height of 3m/10ft, and their spread will be the same on either side. Leave enough room! All side growths should be pinched back in June to six leaves, and again to half way in early spring. Fruit is borne on both the old and new wood.

Pests and Diseases
Cherry slugworm is a green larva which feeds on the leaves in July, causing them to turn brown. Control can be gained by spraying with derris every fortnight from the time fruiting finishes until mid September. *Fruit moth* bores into the fruits as they open, making them unusable; spray with tar oil in January. *Red spider:* see under Plums. *Bacterial canker* appears as yellow circles on the leaves, and eventually spreads to the stems and causes the tree to die. Spray with Bordeaux mixture in November and March to prevent attacks. *Canker:* see under Pears. *Silver leaf:* very serious; see under Plums.

Varieties
'Amber Heart', hardy, reliable, yellow; 'Waterloo', a good pollinator, deep crimson; 'Bigarreau Napoleon', reliable, large red fruits; 'Roundel

A fan-trained peach tree

Heart', good cross-pollinator with 'Waterloo', purple fruits; 'Early Rivers', large black cherries before the end of June; 'Knight's Early Black', black fruits, compact habit.

Peaches

Peaches need a sunny site and shelter from cold winds. If these conditions are available, they can be grown as bush trees in the open, otherwise they are best trained against a sunny wall.

Soil

Planting should be carried out in November, a little bonemeal and plenty of lime rubble being added to the soil. Allow 6m/18ft between fan trees, and 5m/15ft between bushes. Make sure the hole is large enough for the roots to be well spread out, and make sure that the union (point of grafting onto the rootstock) is above soil level. Make sure the trees have plenty of moisture, or the fruits will not swell.

Pruning

Fruit is borne on the previous year's wood, which needs to be well-ripened by the sun. At the end of May, new growth formed by the leader shoots should be cut back by one third, and in mid-summer the tips of the growing shoots should be pinched out. A single wood bud should be retained at the base of each shoot to provide the next season's fruit (wood buds are small and pointed, blossom buds are round and fat). Thin the fruits after the little ones have fallen off to 15cm/6in; thinning is often unnecessary. Pinch out shoots next to a fruit after the second leaf. Peaches do not need pollinators, but if there are not many insects around, it is a good insurance to go over each flower with a camel-hair brush.

Pests and Diseases

Aphis: see Apples. *Red spider:* see Plums. *Scale:* white insects which suck the sap. Spray with tar oil in December or with malathion in early spring. *Bacterial canker:* see Cherries. *Leaf curl:*

a serious disease, usually prevalent in wet years. The leaves curl, turn brown and die, and the disease can spread to the stems. Pick off and burn any infected leaves, and to prevent, spray with lime sulphur before the buds open.

Varieties
'Duke of York' ripens early and produces large dark crimson fruits: 'Early Rivers' is another early variety, yellow skinned with white flesh. 'Peregrine' is a large crimson fruit, very reliable, maturing mid August.

Strawberries

Strawberries prefer a light, well drained soil, and need protecting against frost damage. If the soil is not very well drained, work in some peat, and add plenty of humus–lawn mowings and dead leaves are excellent. Strawberries require equal amounts of nitrogen, phosphorus and potash, and as these are all available in farmyard manure, dressings of this will be beneficial.

Protect strawberries from slug and soil damage

Planting
Plants should be 40cm/16in apart in the rows, and the rows should be 60cm/24in apart. Closer planting encourages mildew. Always purchase stock from a grower who guarantees plants certified by the Ministry of Agriculture. The plants will only crop well for about three years, and if you wish to propagate your own, allow the runners to form in the third season (otherwise cut them off as they appear), cutting off the plantlets which have formed nearest the parent plant, and planting them immediately.

Cultivation
Hoe between the plants in early spring to break up the soil and to allow air and moisture to reach the roots. By the end of April the earliest varieties will be forming blossoms, and some protection should be given if frosts are expected. Give the plants a mulch after the blossom has set–strawy manure is best–and put down clean straw or polythene around the plants to protect the fruits from soil splashing and from slugs.

While the fruit is setting in May and June, make sure the plants have plenty of moisture as otherwise the fruits will not swell. Do not water during harvesting if you wish to freeze the fruit.

Pests and Diseases
Aphis is the worst strawberry pest, feeding on the sap and encouraging virus diseases. Spray with liquid derris in spring before the blossoms open. *Blossom weevil* lays eggs in the blossom, reducing crops considerably: dust the flowers with derris powder as they open, and again a fortnight later. *Tarsonemid mite* lays its eggs in the hearts of the plants as the leaves open; spray with a lime sulphur solution at this time. *Botrytis* is a form of mildew, appearing as a powdery mould on the foliage, and causing the fruit to turn brown and decay. Orthocide dust should be applied in spring, especially in damp districts where the disease will be most prevalent.

Varieties
Early: 'Cambridge Early Pine', round, bright

scarlet; 'Cambridge Regent', resistant to mildew, good for freezing. Second early: 'Cambridge Favourite', heavy cropper, large red fruits; 'Cambridge Vigour', crops well in all soils. Mid season: 'Redgauntlet', compact, excellent flavour; 'Royal Sovereign', very popular with exhibitors. Late: 'Montrose', orange fruits, good flavour; 'Talisman', heavy cropper, tends to be soft. Autumn fruiting: 'Gento', pleasant, acid flavour.

Raspberries

Raspberries flower later than strawberries, so frost is rarely a problem; they do need a spot which is not exposed to cold winds however. Heavy loam is the ideal soil, and plenty of nitrogen should be added.

Plant the canes early in November, always purchasing Ministry of Agriculture certified stock. Plan the canes 45cm/18in apart, and a few days later, cut them back to 20cm/8in above soil level. This will mean no fruit in the first season, but will ensure strong healthy plants thereafter.

Care
Stakes should be set at intervals along the row, and galvanized wires stretched between them at 36cm/15in intervals to a total height of 2m/6ft. Tie the canes to the wires as they reach them. In November, cut the old wood to 3cm/1in above ground, also any weak new shoots, leaving six or eight strong ones on each plant. With autumn fruiting varieties, do not cut the canes back until March.

Pests and Diseases
Aphis can be recognized by swellings on the stems; apply a tar oil wash in January. *Raspberry beetle* is always present as grubs on the fruit, but dusting with derris as the flowers open will reduce attacks. *Raspberry moth* feeds on the fruits and can be prevented from overwintering by tar oil spraying in January. *Cane blight* and *Cane spot* are both fungus diseases which can be reduced by spraying with Bordeaux mixture at leaf burst.

Raspberries

Varieties
Early: 'Lloyd George', excellent flavour, heavy crops; 'Malling Promise', resistant to virus. Mid season: 'Glen Clova', large fruits, sweet and juicy; 'Malling Jewel', large fruits, excellent for freezing and bottling. Late: 'Malling Admiral', virus resistant, heavy cropper; 'Norfolk Giant', immune to all diseases, good for bottling. Autumn fruiting: 'Fallgold', American, yellow berries, good flavour; 'Zeva', hardy, continuing until October.

Gooseberries

Gooseberries like a light well drained soil with plenty of potash added. Plant in autumn, 1.2m/4ft apart. When pruning, cut back drooping varieties to an upwards bud, and those of an upright habit to an outward pointing bud to prevent overcrowding in the centre of the plant.

Pests and Diseases
Aphis: see Raspberries. *Sawfly:* the grubs cause the blossom to bear no fruit. Spray with liquid derris when the blossom opens. *Botrytis:* see Strawberries. *Leaf spot:* brown spots on the leaves, causing them to fall prematurely. Spray with Bordeaux mixture after harvesting the gooseberries.

Varieties
Early: 'Bedford Red', compact, good for small gardens, large deep crimson fruit; 'May Duke', ready to pick in May for cooking, leave till June for dessert. Mid season: 'Careless', very reliable, excellent for bottling, freezing and cooking;

Above: blackcurrants forming
Left: a heavy currant crop

'Leveller', huge yellow berries, spreading habit. Late: 'Rifleman', large crimson fruits, excellent flavour; 'Whinham's Industry', large crimson fruits, suitable for dessert or cooking.

Blackcurrants and Redcurrants

Currants need a sheltered position and plenty of sun. They are deep rooting, so add plenty of humus to the soil when planting, which should be done between November and March. Set the plants 1.5m/5ft apart, and in early March cut back all wood to 8cm/3in above the ground, to build up a sturdy root system.

On established blackcurrants (three years old and more), cut back the older shoots in winter–the best fruit is borne on the new wood. Redcurrants on the other hand bear fruit on the old wood, and all laterals should be cut back to 3cm/1in, and leaders should be tipped.

Pests and Diseases
Gall mite causes big bud, which can eventually kill the plant; spray with lime sulphur in early spring. *Leaf spot* and *Rust* are diseases recognized by brown and orange spots respectively, and can be controlled by spraying with Bordeaux mixture after picking the fruit.

Varieties
Blackcurrants Early: 'Boskoop Giant', sweet and juicy, 'Laxton's Giant', good for bottling. Mid season: 'Blacksmith', heavy cropper; 'Seabrook's Black', compact habit, large fruit. Late: 'Amos Black', heavy crop, thick skins; 'Baldwin', very juicy.

Redcurrants Early: 'Fay's Prolific', neat and compact; 'Jonkheer van Tets', large, sweet, juicy. Mid season: 'Houghton Castle', spreading habit, very sweet. Late: 'Wilson's Long Bunch', spreading, pink berries, good flavour.

18 House Plants and Bottle Gardens

Foliage and flowering house plants are now so well known that they need little introduction. Their popularity has increased enormously over the years since they were introduced about thirty years ago. Flowering pot plants, of course, have been with us for a far longer period, but foliage house plants with their many varieties still seem modern and new mainly due to the wide range of choice. New introductions keep coming out and many old plants are being revived that have almost been lost to commercial cultivation.

In Victorian times there were not so many house plants as we know them today; they were mostly warm greenhouse stove plants. These were brought into the house from the conservatory for short periods and then taken back for resuscitation. Light conditions in the home were very poor and central heating almost unknown at the end of the 19th century. Things have changed a lot since 1945 and now one is used to good heating and excellent light in our homes.

Many of the more recent introductions have been carefully chosen for their ability to thrive and grow well in the home. The ficuses, ivies and philodendrons come immediately to mind and you can add members of the vine family. The most important factor of all, without doubt, is the way you go about watering your plants.

So much depends on various points, such as:
1) The time of year,
2) The variety of plant,
3) The conditions of the room it is growing in, and
4) The type of soil the plant is potted in.

The Time of Year
In the winter time all plants will be going through a semi-dormant period; this means that the roots are resting and far from active, thus requiring NO feed and very modest watering. When in doubt, always withhold the water. Rarely will you see a foliage plant flagging from lack of water during November to February. Make sure you use tepid water during the winter months, but during the rest of the year this is unimportant. So many plants are spoilt during the winter time by being overwatered and the roots become sick and unhealthy. Leaves go dull looking and they will turn yellow. In such cases there is little one can do; watering will kill the plant rather than save it, so the golden rule is to keep it as dry as you dare and gradually the plant, if not too far gone, will come back to life.

A healthy plant, which means a healthy root system, will become active at its roots towards the end of April and continues until August. There are therefore five months of the year when watering can be given more freely.

Feeding is another matter, but these are the months when this can be beneficial. Never feed in the winter months.

The Variety of Plant
Here one must depend on the instructions according to the label. Reputable firms will give careful instructions and one must make sure to read these. The sansevieria (mother in law's tongue) is a variety that needs little water; one of the reasons for this is that they have very fleshy leaves which can store and hold a good water supply. No foliage house plants need

Citrus mitis, the calamondin orange

excessive watering and generally speaking they like to be kept just moist and never wet.

The Conditions of the Room in which they are Growing.

Many rooms depend on gas fires, electric fires or open coal fires. When the room is not in use then heating soon works down to nil. This means that the plants have to cope with considerable extremes of temperatures. When the heating is on the air in the room becomes hot and dry. This is not an ideal condition for plants and it can be improved by bedding a plant down in damp moss or peat. Moisture can then rise through the leaves and create an excellent micro climate of its own. With hot and cold conditions taking over it is far better to water sparingly and remember that when the temperature falls the plant kept on the dry side will suffer far less than if it were wet. Watering in the mornings when all the day is ahead is the correct thing to do. Avoid any watering at night time, even if the plant looks as though it needs water – let it wait until morning.

The Type of Soil Plants are Potted in

In the old days far more soil was used for potting plants and the root system took longer to develop and the water laid longer in the soil as it slowly drained through the potting mixture. Nowadays nurserymen use far more peat, in fact some mixes are nearly all peat. There is nothing against peat, which tends to produce quicker growth, which means faster root action and therefore that the plant will drain more freely. Where the drainage is swift then the plant will ask for and take more water, but beware of overwatering peat because this can quickly turn it sour and any goodness in the mix will be lost.

So much on the subject of watering, which is vital if one is to have healthy plants around. Never let any smooth surfaced leaves get dusty. However correct the watering may be the leaves have to breathe, so wipe them with a damp cloth or sponge on both sides. Leaf shine sprays can be obtained on the market but do use these sparingly because the oils in these preparations can clog the leaf pores and leaf drop will follow.

Light

The majority of the plants we call houseplants are inhabitants of woodland in their wild state, usually of the jungle, and a characteristic of woodland is that the plants are seldom in direct sunlight. This means that although most plants like good light they don't like the bright, unshaded light of a south facing windowsill in hot weather. Neither will they like any windowsill at night in very cold weather when draughts blow in and frost forms on the glass. Give your plants any available light by day in the winter but move them at night. In the summer keep them away from direct sunlight striking through closed windows or scorching may occur.

Generally speaking variegated plants and those with brightly coloured leaves need more light than those with plain, darker leaves.

Feeding and Repotting

If you feel your plant needs feeding there are numerous proprietary foods all of which give directions, but there are a few points to be remembered. Never feed a plant that hasn't a healthy root system. You don't give a rich diet to a sick person and you don't feed a plant that has recently been repotted and whose roots have not yet penetrated the new soil. Also, when the plant is semi-dormant during the winter its roots couldn't possibly take up feed.

Much the same points apply to repotting. Plants will grow well in pots that seem impossibly small but if you feel your plant really needs a larger pot, repot it early in the growing season, in late April or May, when it has the best time of the year to get used to new conditions. Never do it in the winter.

Pests

Houseplants are not too much troubled by pests but red spider is probably the worst offender and the chief cause for leaf troubles on foliage plants. Pests come more quickly and multiply freely when the air is hot and dry around the plant. It is misleading to think the red spider looks like a spider. It does not and it is only the very old ones that have a red colouring. The young ones that do so much damage are white in colour if looked at through a strong magnifying glass. They breed in large quantities very quickly and live on both sides of the leaves, extracting all the moisture.

The cures for most pests are easily obtained from horticultural sundriesmen or garden centres. Read the instructions carefully for the troubles you want to eliminate and never overdo the recommended quantities.

We now move onto some of the most popular houseplants. Under some of the family headings there are many different varieties and those worthy of note will be mentioned. In the case of philodendrons, there are many varieties within this Aracaea family. The list given here is in alphabetical order for ease of reference. Twenty-four houseplants have been listed, but of course there are many, many more than these, but the

The poinsettia, always popular at Christmas

ones mentioned are probably the most suitable and satisfying for amateurs.

Aphelandra

The Aphelandra comes from the Acanthaceae family and is well-known to plant lovers and very popular. It has a spike of yellow green bracts from which small yellow flowers emerge; and also has attractive leaves of deep green with shiny ivory coloured veins. The flowers last for quite a time and then fall, starting from the base of the spike and working up to the tip. When the flowers have gone the bracts are left and remain decorative for a long time. When the spike is finished it should be cut back to a good pair of leaves. New shoots will grow from the leaf joints.

Aphelandras have a strong root action from May to August and being hungry feeders will need an ample supply of water and feed. This, of course, must be eased up from September to April.

Asplenium Nidus Avis

This excellent fern is known as the bird's nest fern and can grow into a large plant but it is generally seen and bought in a pot not larger than 14cm/5½in. It likes to be warm and moist and will not thrive too well in a very hot, dry atmosphere. The fronds (leaves) are a shiny, smooth green, something like the hart's tongue we find in the hedgerows. The soil is not of great importance because the plant is bordering on being an epiphyte, but it is essential that the soil should have the best drainage possible. Like all ferns it likes a shady position but not too dark. Young plants are popular in bottle gardens in which conditions are ideal for this type of fern.

Aralia Sieboldii

Aralia sieboldii, sometimes known as Fatsia japonica, in its green form is very easy to keep in almost any position in the home. The variegated form is more difficult because the creamy, yellow tips on the edges of the finger leaves tend to go brown in the winter time and the plant is very demanding of living conditions. If you go for the all green one, that is easy. A mature plant will produce leaves like a hand with six or seven fingers.

Anthurium Guatemala

Anthurium guatemala is a fine variety for growing as a pot plant, making a nice, compact plant and it is more free flowering than other varieties of anthurium. Anthuriums in the past have been grown mainly for cut flowers and not suitably for potted plants. They needed a high temperature of 21°C/70°F and a humidity that would have been impossible to maintain in the living room. Guatemala was an excellent discovery because it only needs a temperature of 18°C/65°F and ordinary humidity. The orange-red spathe flowers are quite prolific and have a long-lasting life. The leaves are a good green and are spear shaped. The whole proportions of this pot plant are so attractive that it should be high up on a list of plants to go in your home.

A large specimen of *Monstera deliciosa*

Begonia Rex

There are so many different varieties that it is impossible to name them. The best ones to choose are those with a compact habit and with leaves that are on the small side. The colours are outstanding, from many shades of silver through to pinks and reds. Most leaves of the begonia rex are multi-coloured except for some silver ones. None of them like too bright a light and direct sunshine for any length of time will spoil the beauty of the leaf surface which under correct conditions shines like velvet or silk. Potting soil should be a light, open soil with a generous amount of peat mixed in. Propagation is done by cutting up a mature leaf into squares about the size of a large postage stamp and laying the pieces flat on top of the soil in a seedbox. Potting on is not necessary for at least two years–they like to remain in the same pot. When you have to pot them do this in late spring.

Begonia Masoniana

Begonia masoniana, introduced by Mr Maurice Mason in 1952, makes a fine houseplant. The leaves are thick and fleshy and marked with a deep purple cross on a green-grey base, which is covered all over with small points. Never try to sponge the leaves of this plant or any of the rex varieties. If they get dusty, then the only way to clean them is to blow it off.

Bromeliads

Bromeliads are fascinating plants to grow and their flowers last a very long time. We owe these decorative plants to Jules Linden, who found them in South America growing as epiphytes on trees about 250 years ago. They have a vase-like centre cup in which water is stored and provides food for the plants through their leaves. The main feature of the root system under natural conditions in the forest is that they act as an anchor for the plants to hold to the trees. Bromeliads do not mind a dry heat provided the centre cup is kept full of water. Young plants are produced by removing the side shoots from the mother plant.

One of the most popular of the many types of this family is Aechmea rhodocyanea, known also as fasciata. This is a native of South America around Rio de Janeiro, it needs good light, and it is best to buy a plant with the flower half developed so one can enjoy the flowering period for at least two months.

Other varieties of interest to grow are bilbergias, nidulariums, vriesias and ananas (the pineapple).

Bilbergias are fairly well known because they are quick growing and consequently cheap to produce. The leaves are rather ordinary but the spikes of tassel-like hanging flowers of green-blue with its pink bracted stem are very spectacular.

Nidulariums produce small flowers, low down in the vase, looking a little like miniature water lilies on the surface of a pool.

Vriesia, once known as splendens, makes a fine plant with dark bands across its leaves and throws a spike like a flaming spear of vivid red.

The ananas (pineapple) in its variegated form is grown as a pot plant. One can have a fruiting plant after a good many years in a greenhouse, but for eating purposes the common green variety is grown in the fields on the equator line where no frost is possible. The variegated form is most spectacular with its green and cream stripes.

Chlorophytum Comosum Variegatum

One sees the chlorophytum or spider plant in almost every home where plants are grown. The leaves are long and narrow, ivory coloured with green margins. Being highly variegated they need good light and frequent watering in summer but cut down very much in winter time. In summer stems will appear with plume-like tips on which tiny plantlets are produced. These can be removed for cultivation as new plants or pegged down with the plant still attached to the plume stalk in a pot of soil. The chlorophytum makes a fine hanging basket plant.

Crotons

Crotons, also known as codiaeums, are shrub-like plants and come from the spurge family. The common name is Jacob's coat, because the colours of the leaves cover a wide and vivid range of pink, red, yellow, orange and green. Crotons need warm, moist conditions and hate cold and draughty situations. They are not easy to grow unless in perfect conditions.

Cissus Antarctica

Cissus antarctica comes from the vine family. It has dark green leaves, about 5cm/2m across and 10cm/4in long. This is a plant tolerant to all conditions and can cope with strong light or shade. It can be grown into a large plant some 2.5m/8ft in height. The plant can go for two years before it needs potting on.

Dieffenbachia

The best variety to grow is Exotica. This is a compact and a more reasonably sized plant than other varieties of diffenbachias. The leaves are about 15cm/6in long by 8cm/3in wide and are

A croton, or codiaeum

Crotons are members of the spurge family

A variegated ficus, or rubber plant

best described as covered with cream-like marbling and as they mature the cream predominates over the green. A very easy and rewarding plant to grow in the home, but beware of eating a leaf. If this does occur then you are liable to loss of speech for a time; hence its common name of dumb cane.

Dracaena

These plants take a long time to grow to a mature plant and until this has been achieved the leaves start with a poor colouring. When they are mature the leaves become larger and of wonderful colours; cream, pink, black and red. Plants are raised by cutting up the stems in short lengths and being laid on top of a peat bed with good bottom heat.

Ficus

The various varieties of ficus (the rubber plant) come under the fig family and there are some 1,100 species in this category. The ficus decora is the most popular of all, and is well known and makes a very good houseplant. It is easy to grow in the home and will stand fairly low temperatures. Like all foliage plants they take a rest in the winter and it is helpful to realise that during this period the roots become almost dormant and require little help until the milder end of April when watering is necessary and important. If a ficus is healthy it can easily make five new leaves during its growing period.

Ficus benjamina is another very good plant to grow. It is nothing like decora to look at, but makes a fine, small weeping tree, very graceful

Marantas need a warm moist atmosphere

with its many side branches of small, shiny green leaves.

Hedera
The ivy family has many different varieties and only comes from the western hemisphere. The varieties chosen for their decorative value will stand low temperatures but would find it hard to survive frost. Most people think of ivy as in the wild ivy with its long joints, and never self-branching. It is obvious that the self-branching varieties are used for decorative pot plants. When tipped at the growing points they branch rapidly at all joints and make very attractive plants and can be kept well under control by this method. Culture is easy–they are very hardy and will put up with quite a lot of neglect. They will grow in almost any soil and rarely need to be repotted. They can be made to trail or climb up

sticks and like to be kept on the dry side. Overwatering if persistently done will kill the roots.

One of the most popular of all the ivies is the hedera canariensis which is not self branching. When buying a plant check that three or four cuttings have been potted into the one pot because this helps the plant to look nice and bushy with its lovely creamy white and green variegated leaves.

Another variety, lutzii, is an excellent grower and will continue to grow quite a lot in the winter time, the leaves are small and green-grey and yellow in colouring.

Chicago variegated is a very attractive ivy with clean cut markings of green and yellow, small leaves but of excellent shape.

Lastly, the hedera helix, the all green small leaved branching variety is a plant for everyone; inexpensive to buy and very easy to look after. Keep taking out the growing tips and a well shaped, bushy plant will result.

Heptapleurum
This plant was seen in Japan in 1972 and introduced to the western hemisphere as a new house plant. By 1975 it had been reproduced on a considerable scale and became available in modest quantities. The plants' leaves are graceful, finger-shaped with seven finger sections, in a good dark green. The plant can be grown in bush form or as a single stem plant or as a standard tree. This wide choice of methods has made the plant deservedly popular.

Maranta
These must have shade with a fairly moist and warm atmosphere. Excellent plants for ground cover in mixed plantings. All marantas have leaves that give a herringbone effect. The two most popular marantas are kerchoveana, with its leaves of emerald green and chocolate blotches between the veins, and tricolor, by far the most spectacular, with vivid crimson veins with dark green colouring between.

Monstera
The non-climbing variety, deliciosa borsigiana,

is the one usually grown and sold to the public. The leaves characterize quickly into a split leaf from the original plain, heart-shaped leaf. A healthy plant will produce many aerial roots as well as those in the pot; these aerial roots should be trained down the main stem so that they can dive into the soil of the pot. The plant needs careful watering and to be grown in a temperature of 18°C/65°F and it likes semi-shade. Monstera pertusa makes smaller leaves and can be classed as a climber, but it is a slow growing variety. Growing up a moss pole speeds up the growth because the aerial roots like to penetrate into the most moss.

Neanthe Bella
This is a delightful small dwarf palm, slow growing and therefore useful in bottle gardens. This miniature palm has feathery leaves. In the winter, like all palms, it should be kept rather dry. It is an easy house plant which has found favour especially in mixed plantings.

Philodendrons
There are many varieties of philodendron that make excellent house plants but the most popular one of all is scandens. These heart-shaped leaves give it the well-earned common name of sweetheart plant and it can be seen in all the flower shops for Valentine's Day. Other varieties well worth buying are bipinnatifidum, hastatum, emerald gem and tuxla. All these varieties have large leaves compared with scandens and need spacious surroundings to show them off to best advantage.

Peperomias
These small decorative pepper plants with short clusters of leaves are most useful as a small bushy plant. There are quite a few varieties but the best ones are in order, magnoliaefolia, caperata and hederaefolia.

Magnoliaefolia has a strong variegation of green and yellow shiny, fleshy leaves. All peperomias like to be kept on the dry side, too much water will cause rot to set in at the base of the plant. Caperata has the smallest leaves and keeps down to a short bushy plant of about three

One of the many members of the peperomia family

inches high. The leaves are deeply corrugated in a very dark colour. The stalks are pink and it throws up mousetail spikes above the leaves. Another good bottle garden plant, hederaefolia, is much the same, but the leaves are a little larger and of a pale grey colour and slightly undulating.

Pilea
Known as the aluminium plant, it came from Indo-China in the late 1930s. Its leaves are oval in shape with dark green colouring, but patches of silver take charge of the overall colour effect which is silver grey. The original plant was inclined to become leggy, but improvements have been made and the variety nana has taken over. Pileas like either semi-shade or a fairly well lit position. They like to be kept moist and should never get really dry. Another excellent bushy plant for anyone's collection of house plants.

Rhoicissus
Member of the vine family, hence its tendrils which help it to climb up a stick. The leaves have a beautiful dark green colouring and have a high, glossy shine. During the early spring, the growing tips should be stopped and bushy growth will result. Apart from making a good climbing plant it will also make a handsome bushy trailer. Keep it away from excessive sunshine because it will tend to yellow and lose its gloss.

Sansevieria
Everyone calls this mother in law's tongue because of the sharp pointed upright leaves. This is probably the one plant that needs far less water than any other houseplant. Even in the spring and summer watering should be very much on the sparse side. The leaves in the centre are grey-green with the margins of yellow stripes. The upright growth of the leaves come from a rhizome which grows under the soil surface of the pot. Sansevierias need, if to do well, a well lit position but they will survive in a shady situation. In the winter monthly watering

will suffice and a little more in late spring and summer.

Tradescantia
Everyone knows the quick growing tradescantia—a cheap plant to buy. The variety Rochford's quicksilver is quite the best one to grow. The leaves are more oval than other varieties, with vivid silver stripes on an emerald green base. Like all tradescantias it needs stopping at least twice through the growing period. They all need to be kept fairly moist. With the exception of Rochford's quicksilver all other varieties tend to grow shoots with plain green leaves; these must be removed as soon as they can be dealt with, otherwise the all green will soon take over the whole of the plant. Tradescantias like to grow out of the pot leaving the centre bare, so put some more cuttings into the middle of the pot. Other good varieties are zebrina, silver and tricolor.

Bottle gardens
These containers will grow house plants well and are very popular with all sections of the community, especially for the aged and those who have to remain rather static in life who can find an added pleasure in having a bottle garden near so that they can watch the plants growing under ideal conditions.

To plant a bottle garden you need a large bottle or carboy, the latter being preferable. Fill the container with a fairly rich growing mix, about 20cm/8in deep and add a little charcoal which will help to keep the soil sweet. To get the soil into the container, pour it through a paper funnel to the base. This will avoid the sides of the carboy getting covered with soil. When the soil is prepared, the best planting method is to use two spoons fixed to the end of two long sticks. A table fork can act as a rake in the same way and a cotton reel pushed tightly onto the end of a stick is useful to firm down the soil.

Always choose slow growing plants so that the bottle will not become an overgrown mass of plants in a short space of time. Useful plants are peperomias, marantas, hoya carnosa variegata,

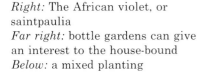

Right: The African violet, or saintpaulia
Far right: bottle gardens can give an interest to the house-bound
Below: a mixed planting

small leaved ivies, fittonias, cryptanthus, small leaved begonia rex, asplenium nidus and other slow growing ferns.

Plants in a carboy like a light position but *not* direct sunshine. A few well chosen stones or tiny rocks will add interest. Small pieces of bark also can be used to good effect. An electric lamp placed above a bottle garden looks good and the plants will enjoy the additional illumination.

If the bottle is firmly corked once it has been planted the plants will grow very successfully but the glass will be coated with moisture and will spoil the view of the plants. If kept like this watering would never be needed again but to enjoy the planting a small amount of ventilation should be given to clear the glass sides. A small amount of water will be required from time to time under these conditions.

On the whole it is best to avoid using flowering plants because it is difficult to remove the flowers when they are finished. The only flowering plant I would suggest is the Saintpaulia (African violet) which is easy to care for; remove the flowers as they fade.

19 Pests and Diseases

Just as there is an infinite range of cultivated and natural plants, so too, is there a myriad of insects and minute life in the form of fungal and bacterial diseases, which depend on plants for their existence.

Left to their own devices, a balance is usually struck between the plants and their hosts, but there is a constant ebb and flow with the resurgence of a particular pest or disease overtaking the plants and vice-versa.

The need to keep all garden pesticides in a safe place cannot be emphasized too strongly and still more important, use them according to the directions supplied with them.

The Main Diseases and Pests of Vegetables

Crop	Pests/ Diseases	Description	Control
Beans, broad	Black fly (Aphis fabae and other aphids)	Very prevalent and damaging by restricting growth.	In gardens, pinch out tops.
Brassicas (broccoli, Brussels sprouts, cabbage, cauliflowers, radish, savoys, turnips)	Clubroot *(Plasmodiophora brassicae)*	A slime mould or fungus invading and distorting the root tissue causing inability of the root to extract water and nutrients. Symptoms: wilting of plants, especially cabbage and cauliflower.	Heavy liming of growing area in spring to give a pH of about 7. Puddle the roots of plants prior to transplanting in a paste of calomel dust. Crop rotation and the avoidance of all brassicas in extreme cases is necessary.
	Cabbage aphis *(Brevicoryne brassica)*	Effects are typical of those caused by sucking pests–distortion and dwarfing.	Spray early and persistently with varied chemicals to avoid build up of disease within the pest. Use derris and pyrethrum.
	Cabbage caterpillars	Collectively known as cabbage butterflies, the eggs are laid from April onwards on the underside of the leaves.	Control measures are becoming less effective due to rapid build up of resistant strains of root fly. Best chemicals for control are (HCH) chloufenvinphos.

Above: the cabbage white butterfly
Right: caterpillars feeding on a
courgette leaf

Crop	Pests/ Diseases	Description	Control
Brassicas (Contd)	Cabbage root fly (*Erioischia Hylemyia brassicae*)	Causes wide destruction, especially to cabbage, cauliflowers and sprouts. Pests overwinter in the soil as pupae and flies appear round about mid April (or later if the weather is cold).	Control measures are becoming less effective due to rapid build-up of resistant strains of root fly. Best chemicals for control are Aldrin, HCH and chlorfenuinphos.
Carrots	Carrot fly (*Psila rosae*)	The female fly lays its eggs in clusters or singly in cracks close to the carrot. Where thinning is carried out, the holes left are ideal repositories for the eggs.	A range of chemicals are used, including both seed dressings (HCH with captan or thiram) dusted on to the seed *before* it is sown, and this is probably the best and safest method for the amateur.
Celery	Carrot Fly (*Psila rosae*)	see carrots	Malathion (as for carrot fly) is likely to give a measure of control.
Leeks	Rust (*Puccinea porri*)	Orange spots on leaves causing death of leaves and stunting growth are typical symptoms.	No really effective control, but reduced by copper, maneb or zineb.

Crop	Pests/ Diseases	Description	Control
Onions	Onion fly (*Delia Hylemyia antigua*)	The adult fly, like the common house fly in appearance, lays its eggs in stem or leaves at ground level in May and early June, giving rise to small grubs in 3 days. Grubs eat into the base of the bulb.	Control lies in seed dressing with dieldrin. Note: Calomel dust can be used around the plants in the rows and can also be used for seed dressing.
Peas	Fusarium foot rot (*Fusarium solani*) (*F.pisi*)	Lower leaves begin to turn brown and if stems are examined at ground level, they will be seen to be brown and pinched in.	Drazoxolon or thiram seed dressings help and many seedsmen carry this out at no extra cost. Rotation is also helpful.
Potatoes	Blight (*Phytophthora infestans*)	A serious disease, especially in wet summers, when foliage is prematurely destroyed reducing total yield.	Do not plant doubtful tubers.
	Virus diseases	Potatoes can be affected by virus diseases, some transmitted or spread by aphids, others in the soil, and by pests such as eelworm. Virus disease presence in planting stock is one reason why the Certification Scheme for seed potatoes was implemented. Do not keep self-saved seed too long, it is better to buy new seed from a reliable source.	
	Potato root eelworm (*Heterodera rostochiensis*) (also known as Potato cyst eelworm)	A persistent pest because of the method which the larvae 'rest', which is a cyst. In a severe attack, the foliage yellows and dies back.	Crop rotation is the best answer. If eelworm levels are low, plenty of organic matter and gross feeding can enable crops to be grown to a reasonable level despite their presence.
	Slugs	No other single pest causes so much harm in the vegetable garden as slugs, and this is true of the potato. Tubers are holed irrevocably and the whole crop can be ruined.	Early lifting is best, especially in a wet season.

The hedgehog is the gardener's friend – he eats many pests

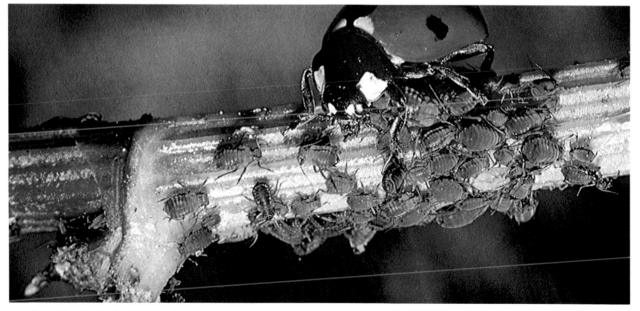

Another friend, the ladybird, who feeds on greenfly and aphids

Diseases and Pests of Fruit

Crop	Pests/ Diseases	Symptoms	Control
Apple	Apple mildew (*Podosphaera leucotricha*)	Leaves, blossom trusses and new shoots can all be affected by white fluffy mould, which reduces and distorts growth.	Systematic fungicide (thiophanate-methyl) or dinocap at pink bud stage (late April-early May). Prune out badly mildewed shoots before this. Follow up with further sprays at intervals of 7–14 days.
	Apple scab (*Venturia inaequalis*)	A very common trouble causing spotting of leaves, splits and scars on fruit rendering it useless.	The same spraying programme as for mildew is effective using systemic fungicide (captan) at 10 day intervals.
	Apple canker (*Nectria galligena*)	A vicious and serious disease attacking branches, causing scars and eventual die-back.	Avoid leaving large open pruning cuts. DNC sprays plus mercury at bud break stage.
	Aphid species (*Rhopalosiphum insertum, Dysaphis plantaginea Aphis pomi, Dysaphis devecta*)	All cause distortion of leaves and shoots and restrict growth.	Spray with winter wash (tar oil or DNOC). If bad attack occurs in spring or summer, use dimethoate, malathion or derris.
	Apple sawfly (*Hoplocampa testudinea*)	A nasty pest. Fruit is mined by caterpillars.	A wide range of chemical can be used, including systemic insecticides and BHC, usually about 7 days after petal fall.
Peach	Red spider sps. (*glasshouse red spider*) (*Tetranychus urticae*)	Foliage hard, parchment-like with yellow mottling on upper surface, becoming completely yellow.	Resistance may occur as in aphids and treatment should be varied. Many acarides are available including (on seedlings) sprays of dimethoate. Remove old crop immediately fruit finished to prevent hibernation of mites.
Plum Damson	Silver leaf (*Stereum purpureum*)	A bad disease which is always a risk when plums are grown. Leaves go silver hue (usually July/August)–one branch on side of a tree to begin with) followed by death of branch.	Disease spread by spores. Prune only in summer June/July/August. Paint over cuts with tar oil wash or paint. Remove and burn dead branches by July 15th.

Crop	Pests Diseases	Description	Control
Currants: Black White Red	Reversion	A virus disease spread by bud mite and possibly other pests. At grape stage of flowering, colour of flower seems darker, but more significant is reduction of veins on leaves, causing them to alter shape.	No control, other than avoidance of cuttings from infected bushes.
	Blackcurrant gall mite (Big bud mite) *(Cecidophyopsis ribis)*	No other pest of fruit is perhaps as well known as this. Tiny mites infest leaf scales preventing buds opening, which results in small blackened buds.	Lime sulphur applied at the grape stage is the best general recommendation.
Gooseberry	American gooseberry mildew *(Sphaerotheca mors-uvae)*	White hairy growth on shoots, leaves and fruit.	Spray at first open flower stage with benomyl or dinocap.
	Gooseberry sawfly caterpillar *(Pteronidea ribesii)*	Often considered the worst pest of the gooseberry. Green caterpillars spotted with black dots and black heads start to eat leaves in April/May.	Azinphos-methyl, fenitrothion, derris and malathion are recommended as soon as pests are seen.
Raspberry	Raspberry moth ('Borer') *(Lampronia rubiella)*	Dead cane tip if examined at end of April or early May will be found to contain red grubs or brown chrysalis. As the base of bud is eaten away, canes die.	Spray with tar oil and DNOC winter wash. In April, spray with carbaryl.
Strawberries	Botrytis or grey mould *(Botrytis cinerea)*	Total loss of fruit due to botrytis grey mould is very high, especially in moist areas or a wet season.	Control measures should be taken *before* attack starts. Chemicals recommended are: benomyl, captan, and thiram. Directions given with the product must be followed.

Pests and Diseases in the Greenhouse

Crop	Pests/ Diseases	Description	Control
Cucumber	Grey mould (*Botrytis cinerea*)	Water-soaked lesions at nodes and at side shoots and leaf scars. Fruits rotted.	Remove infected tissue. Reduce humidity.
	Stem and roots rots (*Rhizoctonia sp, Pythium sp, Phytopthora sp*)	Light brown (Rhizoctonia) or dark brown (Pythium/Phytophthora) lesions at stem bases of seedlings or young plants. Rotting of the shoots.	Sterilize soil in seed boxes and in beds. If Rhizoctonia occurs, apply quintozene dust to surface of bed and rake in.
	Red core (*Phytophthora fragariae*)	A very serious problem in infected soils.	Long rotation the only answer.
Tomato	Damping-off rot and foot rots (*Rhizoctonia solani, Pythium spp. Phytophthora spp*)	Collapse of seedlings or young plants at soil level. Roots may be rotted.	Sterilize seed boxes, pots and compost. Ensure clean water supply. Drench soil surface with Cheshunt compound.
	Leaf mould (*Cladosporium fulvum*)	Yellow patches on upper surface of leaves with brown or purplish velvety fur of fungus on lower surface.	Avoid conditions of high humidity (ie ventilate and give a little heat to create a buoyant atmosphere). Give reasonable space between plants.
	Wilts (*verticillium albo-atrum, V. dahliae, Fusarium oxysporum F.lycopersici and F.redolens*)	Yellowing and/or wilting of leaves progressively up the plant.	Hygiene and soil sterilization essential. Stem base drench (1 pint/plant) with benomyl after planting may reduce infection. Grow resistant varieties.
	Greenback	The shoulder of the fruit stays green. Ailsa Craig and its offspring are susceptible.	Do not over-defoliate. Shade in extreme cases when very hot weather persists. Increase the application of potash.

Pests and Diseases of Trees

Diseases	Symptoms	Control (if any)
Chafer beetles (Cock chafer–*Melonontha vulgaris*) (Garden chafer–*Thyllopertha horticola*) (Rose chafer–*Cetonia aurata*)	Seen in swarms in spring and early summer and especially abundant in vicinity of woods and heaths where the ground tends to be of the lightest nature and dry. Attack a great variety of trees, shrubs and other hard-wooded plants. Larvae feed on the roots of grass and other plants.	Very difficult to control and involves hand picking, the application of naphthalene, trapping with turf and the protective spraying of foliage of trees and shrubs with various insecticides.
Cutworms (Many different species which are larvae of various moths)	Attack a wide range of trees and shrubs, especially at young stage. Eat lower leaves and bite into roots.	Poison bait is effective, also derris and BHC dusts. The destruction of weeds in borders and waste ground in vicinity of garden is also helpful.
Tree Root Rot fungus (*Armillaria mellea*)	One of the most commonest and most destructive of fungi to trees. Fungus first develops on stumps and dead roots of old trees then spreads to young trees. The mycelium travels quickly through the ground.	Remove and burn all roots from the ground before planting young trees. Check mycelium by digging a trench 45cm/18in wide and 60–90cm/2–3ft deep to cut off infected area.

Left: a chafer beetle

Diseases Which Attack Many Plants Out of Doors and Under Protection

Disease	Symptoms	Control (if any)
Aphids or 'Greenfly'. Green, black and various coloured winged and wingless pests, many of which are described under specific plants or crops.	The leaf-curling aphid produces extreme curling of leaves. Green apple aphids distort shoots and stems. Tulip aphid causes distortion of foliage, etc.	Often impossible to control effectively on large trees or shrubs. Malathion is useful but it is better to interchange insecticidal materials to avoid build up of resistance within the pest.
Birds	Pull seedlings out and eat leaves. Eat grass seed.	Netting on small scale. Bird scarers, or use of repellants.
Common black ant (*Lasius niger*)	Spread pests such as mealy bugs and disturb seed after it has been sown.	Carbon disulphide inserted into the nests is highly effective.
Damping off and root rots (*Pythium spp, Rhizoctonia solani, Phytophthora spp, Thielaviopsis basicola*)	Seedlings and plants keel over and die at a fairly early age or stage of growth.	More common under glass than out of doors because of humid atmosphere. Remove diseased, moribund or dead tissue and destroy. Avoid overcrowding. Under glass give adequate ventilation and warmth to create a buoyant atmosphere. Spray or dust with captan or thiram. Spray with benomyl or use tecnazene smoke under glass. Dichlofluanid may also be used.
Grey mould (*Botrytis cinerea*)	Soft rotting of the tissues, which later become covered with smoky grey fur of fungal growth. Spots may occur on leaves and flowers which later rot.	
Leaf spots (Various species of fungi including *Septoria, Cercospora, Phyllosticta* etc)	May coalesce to form larger areas of dead tissue.	Remove and burn affected leaves. Protectant sprays with copper or dithiocarbamate fungicides may be helpful. Check for any phytotoxicity before using extensively.
Mice	Stems and foliage, bulbs and tubers nibbled.	Use traps and/or poison baits.
Stem and bulb eelworm (*Ditylenchus dipsaci*)	Nearly all soft-leaved plants are susceptible. Eggs are laid in the tissues of the plant and develop into larvae which causes the leaves to become narrow and stunted.	Extremely difficult to control. Various potent chemicals can be used but it is best to contact your garden centre to check what is available.
Springtails (*Collembola*)	Seedlings and young plants with pin holes or scraping of surface of foliage. Springtails (minute white or colourless wingless insects) present in large numbers when soil floated in bucket of water.	Apply gamma-BHC dust to soil, or drench with gamma-BHC or malathion.

Disease	Symptoms	Control (if any)
Whitefly *(Trialeurodes vaporariorum)* (Mainly under protective cultivation)	Small adults with white wings, larvae stage scalelike. Adults fly away in clouds when foliage disturbed. Found in large numbers in young plants and growing point of old plants.	Spray with malathion or diazinon. Biological control possible but not always practical.
Wireworms (Several species) (Most common are *Athous haemorrhoidalis* and *Agriotes lineatus*)	Larvae of the click beetle. Attack roots, stems, bulbs, corms, tubers and rhizomes of a wide range of plants. Generally brown in colour. They feed first on decaying root and vegetable matter but as they grow they attack many plants.	Wireworms are universally present in newly broken grassland and a useful cleaning crop is the potato, which should be lifted early and the wireworm riddled tubers destroyed. Mustard as a green crop sown in July and dug in when about 7.5cm/3in high is also useful for control.

Roses

Disease	Symptoms	Control (if any)
Black Spot	Very much a problem now with the lack of sulphur in the atmosphere as the effect of the 'Clean Air Act' has spread over the country . Leaves progressively develop black spots. As the fungus develops, leaves wither and drop. Worst in a wet summer.	Spray with mancozeb, zineb or dichlofluanid. Ground should be sprayed in spring with colloidal copper or a household disinfectant. Nurserymens' catalogues usually list varieties resistant to black spot.

Above: black spot on rose leaves

Index